American Home Front in World War II

Biographies

American Home Front in World War II

Biographies

Richard C. Hanes
and
Kelly Rudd

Allison McNeill,
Project Editor

U·X·L
An imprint of Thomson Gale, a part of The Thomson Corporation

Detroit • New York • San Francisco • San Diego • New Haven, Conn. • Waterville, Maine • London • Munich

American Home Front in World War II: Biographies

Richard C. Hanes and Kelly Rudd

Project Editor
Allison McNeill

Permissions
Emma Hull

Imaging and Multimedia
Robyn Young, Lezlie Light, Dan Newell

Product Design
Michelle Dimercurio, Pamela Galbreath

Composition
Evi Seoud

Manufacturing
Rita Wimberley

LIBRARY OF CONGRESS CATALOGING-IN-PUBLICATION DATA

Hanes, Richard Clay, 1946–
American home front in World War II. Biographies / Richard C. Hanes and Kelly Rudd; Allison McNeill, project editor.
     p. cm. – (American home front in World War II reference library)
    Includes bibliographical references and index.
    ISBN 0-7876-7652-7
1. World War, 1939-1945–United States. 2. World War, 1939-1945–Biography. 3. United States–Biography. I. Title: Biographies. II. Rudd, Kelly, 1954- III. McNeill, Allison. IV. Title. V. Series.
D769.1.H37 2004
973.917'092'2–dc22
                                             2004009393

This title is also available as an e-book.
ISBN 0-7876-9385-5 (Set)
Contact your Gale sales representative for ordering information.

Printed in the United States of America
10 9 8 7 6 5 4 3 2 1

Contents

Introduction

Many people who lived on the American home front during World War II (1939–45; U.S. involvement 1941–45) proclaimed the period as "the best of times and worst of times." In the 1930s the United States and much of the rest of the world had been in the throes of the Great Depression. The Depression was marked by dramatically slowed business activity, high unemployment, and, for a significant portion of the population, much hunger. In the United States, society seemed, at times, to be falling apart as violent labor conflicts, food riots, and race riots punctuated the 1930s. Change came in 1940 as the United States began gearing up for a war that was already raging in Europe. As industries began receiving sizable government contracts to produce war materials, good-paying jobs once again became available for anyone who wanted to work. On December 7, 1941, the Japanese surprised and shocked the United States with a deadly attack on U.S. military bases at Pearl Harbor, Hawaii. Immediately an overwhelming spirit of patriotic fervor consumed America. A common cause and a common enemy became well-defined.

The war years were the "best of times" because the war effort united Americans as never before. The factories were humming, men and women were working and earning livable wages, even rationing of food and gasoline was viewed as necessary for the push to victory. At the same time, the "worst" aspect of the early 1940s involved separation from loved ones as millions joined the military and went overseas to fight for their country. Americans held their collective breath until their sons, husbands, brothers, and even daughters returned to the home front.

The United States was clearly a different nation in 1942 than the previous decade. Just about everything aspect of society was affected. Changes came in employment, living locations, and in driving and eating habits. Millions of new jobs caused personal income to rise dramatically and an improved standard of living. Taking advantage of new employment, individuals and whole families migrated to the war industry centers on each coast and the Great Lakes region. Millions of American men joined the military service and left for far off places. Change also came as everyone on the home front pitched in to do their part for the war effort. They volunteered for civil defense duties, complied with food and gasoline rationing, planted "victory gardens," and collected scrap metal and rubber tires that contained materials needed in producing war materials. Cities staged practice air raid drills with blackouts, as volunteer air raid wardens patrolled the streets and neighborhoods. Citizens, fearing spies and saboteurs, kept a vigilant watch, viewing anyone with an accent with suspicion. Housewives shopped with ration coupons and adapted recipes to find substitutes for sugar and meat, which were rationed items. Families readjusted transportation priorities to make do on four gallons of gasoline a week. Citizens on the home front also helped feed the nation and free up a portion of commercially grown fruits and vegetables for shipment overseas. Over twenty million home gardens, known as victory gardens, were planted. They provided one-third of all vegetables eaten in America. Youth joined the effort by rounding up scrap materials in the form of discarded pots and pans, bedsprings, tin cans, and rubber tires for use in manufacturing war materials.

The entertainment industry participated in the war effort as well. Hollywood directors produced war documentaries aimed at bolstering the wave of patriotism. New movie releases showed Japanese and German characters as villainous, while promoting traditional American cultural values and creating American heroes. Celebrities contributed to war bond drives, leading to the sales of millions of dollars of bonds. Others volunteered at canteens where servicemen could stop for food and entertainment before departing for overseas assignments. Still others enlisted in the regular armed services or volunteered in civilian defense roles.

Through the major government and private industry mobilization efforts and the patriotic fervor of the population, the American home front became the leading industrial and agricultural producer in the world. Existing factories were converted from production of civilian consumer goods, such as cars, toasters, alarm clocks, and refrigerators, to wartime materials such as warplanes, tanks, guns, ammunition, and military trucks. Major new factories were built, as well as massive new shipyards where thousands of freight transports, known as "Liberty" ships, were produced. U.S. industry produced almost three hundred thousand warplanes, over eighty-six thousand tanks, and almost twelve thousand ships between 1941 and 1945. Long workweeks became commonplace for war industry workers.

Corporations and farmers saw their investments grow. Corporate assets almost doubled as the government guaranteed profits on war production. Farmers also saw their prosperity rise to new heights by growing food for the armies of the Allied forces. Big business and military services formed a long lasting powerful alliance known as the military-industrial complex. The alliance would influence U.S. foreign policy and industrial production for decades following the war.

Despite the vastly improved economic outlook, for some Americans not all was rosy. Racial discrimination increased. With war quickly expanding in Europe in 1940, Congress passed the Smith Act requiring four million aliens, those not yet U.S. citizens, but living in America, to register with U.S. authorities. Following the bombing of Pearl Harbor, President Franklin D. Roosevelt signed an order labeling German, Italian, and Japanese immigrants as enemy aliens. Though restrictions on Germans and Italians would soon ease, Japanese aliens experienced harsh discrimination. In the spring of 1942 the U.S. government hastily rounded up some 112,000 Japanese aliens, as well as Japanese Americans with full U.S. citizenship, from their homes and businesses. They were transported to remote detention camps where they were held for the remainder of the war. Meanwhile their constitutionally protected rights were trampled.

Black Americans experienced much needed gains in the newly expanded job markets, but only after non-minorities were fully employed and labor shortages had become critical. Some new opportunities in the military services also opened for blacks. However the armed services remained racially segregated, as was civilian life in much of the home front. Triggered by job discrimination and severe housing shortages in the war industry centers, violent race riots broke out on the home front in 1943. The worst racial rioting occurred in Detroit, Michigan, where thirty-four were killed and seven hundred injured.

As with minorities, women found new opportunities in jobs never available before, such as factory assembly-line jobs. "Rosie the Riveter" became a mythical caricature symbolic of all women who took jobs in war industries. Millions of women entered the workforce during the war years. By late 1944 women made up some 40 percent of the workforce in aircraft factories and 12 percent in shipyards. Much of the wartime home front gains proved short-lived. Women were expected to leave their jobs at the war's end so that returning veterans could find work to support their families.

Though the home front worker had money to spend, fewer goods were available to purchase because factory production and raw materials were directed to military use. No new automobiles, radios, or appliances were produced during the war. The government introduced a rationing system to ensure fair distribution of limited goods. Rationed items and materials included sugar, coffee, meat, canned goods, leather shoes, and dairy products. Gasoline for automobiles was rationed in a complex system based on demonstrated need.

The most difficult home front shortage to overcome was the shortage of housing. Twenty million Americans relocated to industrial centers or military bases only to find little available housing. Because of war needs for war materials, few new houses were built.

With little to spend money on, savings grew and personal debt declined. The government encouraged citizens to invest their extra funds in war bonds to help finance the very expensive war effort. The war bond drives served to keep home front Americans involved in actively supporting the war. Congress also passed and instituted the modern federal income tax system. Forty million Americans were paying income tax by 1945, up from just five million in 1939.

By 1943 the war became a test of will and endurance. Most affected by war on the home front were those with loved ones in the military service, particularly those serving overseas. American casualties mounted as the war continued, with the most deaths occurring in the last twelve months. Ultimately fifteen million Americans served in the wartime military. Of those, three hundred thousand were killed and seven hundred thousand injured. As a reward to those who served in the military, the government introduced sweeping programs of financial assistance amounting to $100 billion in benefits for millions of war veterans and their families. The funds provided a significant boost to the U.S. postwar economy as veterans used the funds to buy homes and fund their education.

Early 1945 brought a rapid sequence of events. Germany surrendered on May 7. The following day became known as V-E Day for Victory in Europe. The Japanese surrendered on August 14, and the following day became known as V-J Day for Victory Over Japan. The war's end in mid-1945 brought wild jubilation on the American home front. As time passed and new generations grew up, the prominent place of World War II became fixed in U.S. history. Despite vast destruction of parts of Europe and Asia, the United States home front, with the exception of Pearl Harbor, was spared any physical harm. Many Americans later looked nostalgically back at World War II as a simpler time of patriotic unity and adventure.

Richard C. and Sharon M. Hanes

Reader's Guide

American Home Front in World War II: Biographies presents the life stories of twenty-six individuals who played key roles on the American home front while the nation was at war from 1941 to 1945. Individuals from all walks of life are included. Some held prominent national roles in guiding America through the war, others were among the millions who eagerly did their share in contributing to the war effort. Profiled are well-known figures such as President Franklin D. Roosevelt, First Lady Eleanor Roosevelt, Secretary of War Henry Stimson, painter Norman Rockwell, social activist A. Philip Randolph, industrialists Donald Douglas and Henry Kaiser, entertainers Betty Grable and Dorothy Lamour, movie director Frank Capra, and journalist Elmer Davis, as well as lesser-known individuals such as industrial worker Peggy Terry, artist and author Mine Okubo, physicist Elda Anderson, and labor leader Luisa Moreno.

Features

The entries in *American Home Front in World War II: Biographies* contain sidebar boxes that highlight topics of special interest related to the profiled individual. Each entry also offers a list of additional sources students can go to for more information. More than fifty black-and-white photographs illustrate the material. The volume begins with a timeline of important events in the history of home front America during World War II and a "Words to Know" section that introduces students to difficult or unfamiliar terms (terms are also defined within the text). The volume concludes with a general bibliography and a subject index so students can easily find the people, places, and events discussed throughout *American Home Front in World War II: Biographies*.

American Home Front in World War II Reference Library

American Home Front in World War II: Biographies is only one component of the three-part U•X•L American Home Front in World War II Reference Library. The other two titles in this set are:

- ***American Home Front in World War II: Almanac*** (one volume) presents, in thirteen chapters, a comprehensive overview of events and everyday life that occurred within the United States while the nation was at war from 1941 to 1945. The volume concentrates on the actual events related to the World War II effort rather than simply relating all general happenings of the time period. Coverage includes the sweeping mobilization of American industry, women entering the work force, the effects of war on everyday life, preparations for a changed postwar world, and the legacies of the home front in World War II that were felt throughout the twentieth century .

- ***American Home Front in World War II: Primary Sources*** (one volume) tells the story of the American home front in the words of the people who lived and shaped it. Approximately thirty excerpted documents provide a wide range of perspectives on this period of history. Included are excerpts from presidential addresses and proclamations; government pamphlets; magazine articles; and reflections by individuals who lived through the tumultuous times.

A cumulative index of all three titles in the U•X•L American Home Front in World War II Reference Library is also available.

Dedication

The *American Home Front in World War II* volumes are dedicated to our new grandson Luke Clay Hanes. May he and his generation be spared the trauma and ravages of war.

Special Thanks

Kelly Rudd contributed importantly to the *Biographies* volume. Catherine Filip typed much of the manuscript for the *Primary Sources* volume. Constance Carter, head of the Library of Congress science research department, assisted in searching out primary source materials.

Comments and Suggestions

We welcome your comments on *American Home Front in World War II: Biographies* and suggestions for other topics to consider. Please write: Editors, *American Home Front in World War II: Biographies,* U•X•L, 27500 Drake Rd. Farmington Hills, Michigan 48331-3535; call toll free: 1-800-877-4253; fax to (248) 699-8097; or send e-mail via http://www.gale.com.

Timeline of Events

October 1929 The Great Depression arrives, leading to high unemployment rates and social unrest; over the next few years the Depression spreads worldwide, hitting Germany particularly hard.

September 18, 1931 Japan invades and occupies Manchuria to gain access to its natural resources, beginning Japan's military expansion in the Far East through the next decade.

January 30, 1933 Adolf Hitler becomes Germany's head of government.

March 4, 1933 Franklin D. Roosevelt is inaugurated as the thirty-second president of the United States.

1935 Germany introduces a military draft and begins mobilizing its industries to produce military materials, including tanks and war planes.

October 3, 1935 Italy invades Ethiopia and gains control by May 1936.

July 7, 1937 Japan invades China, capturing many of its major cities including its capital, Peking (Beijing).

March 12, 1938 Germany announces a union with Austria.

October 15, 1938 Germany gains control of part of Czechoslovakia, beginning its military expansion in Europe.

1939 Pocket Book Company introduces the paperback book, which will become highly popular through the war, selling 40 million in 1943 alone.

September 1, 1939 Germany invades Poland, thereby starting World War II. Several nations, including Britain and France, declare war on Germany two days later; President Roosevelt declares U.S. neutrality in the following days.

September 5, 1939 Congress revises the Neutrality Acts, ending the ban of sales of military supplies to foreign nations; the United States establishes a cash and carry program to sell war materials to Great Britain.

September 8, 1939 President Roosevelt issues a limited national emergency declaration and creates the War Resources Board (WRB) to begin planning for war.

1940 Roosevelt creates the Office of Emergency Management (OEM), located in the White House, to oversee war preparations.

March 16, 1940 Roosevelt, in a speech, asks for construction of 50,000 warplanes in preparation for war and sale to Britain.

April 9, 1940 Germany begins a military assault on Western Europe, first invading Denmark and Norway, eventually leading to the fall of France on June 22.

June 1940 Dr. Vannevar Bush meets with President Roosevelt, leading to the creation of the National Defense Research Committee (NRDC) to coordinate technological research benefiting advanced military equipment.

June 28, 1940 Congress passes the Alien Registration Act, more commonly known as the Smith Act, one week after the fall of France, making it illegal to advocate the overthrow of the U.S. government.

July 10, 1940 Henry Stimson becomes U.S. Secretary of War, appointed by President Roosevelt.

July 10, 1940   The German bombing of Britain begins; it lasts for eight months. Italy declares war on France and Great Britain.

September 15, 1940   Congress passes the first peacetime military draft in U.S. history.

September 27, 1940   Germany, Italy, and Japan form a military alliance.

November 5, 1940   With the public fearful of looming war, President Roosevelt is elected to an unprecedented third term in office.

December 1940   Industrialist Henry Kaiser and two partners win a government contract to build thirty cargo ships for the British, the first of many shipbuilding government contracts Kaiser will receive through the war years, building one-third of the nation's cargo ships for the war.

December 29, 1940   In a Fireside Chat, Roosevelt delivers his "Arsenal of Democracy" speech calling for greater efforts in supporting the war against Germany.

1941   Physicist Elda E. Anderson joins the staff at the Office of Scientific Research and Development at Princeton University, leading to her participation in the Manhattan Project in 1943, the program to develop the atomic bomb.

January 1941   Roosevelt creates the Office of Production Management (OPM) to spur industrial war mobilization.

January 1941   A. Philip Randolph calls for a national march of at least ten thousand black Americans on Washington set for July 1.

January 6, 1941   Artist Norman Rockwell is so inspired by President Roosevelt's "Four Freedoms" speech that he begins creating a series of highly popular paintings based on the four freedoms that help sell over $133,000,000 in government war bonds.

February 4, 1941   United Service Organizations (USO) is created to provide entertainment to American troops; it establishes Camp Shows, Inc., through which entertainers volunteer to perform for military servicemen, amounting to over 428,000 shows by 1947.

March 1941   The National Defense Mediation Board is formed to resolve labor disputes in industry and to ease the process of war mobilization.

March 6, 1941   The first houses in the Linda Vista housing development in San Diego, California, are completed for war industry workers; 16,000 residents are housed here by April 1943.

March 11, 1941   Congress passes the Lend-Lease Act, authorizing the United States to lend Britain and other nations fighting Germany money to purchase or lease military equipment and supplies from U.S. industry; the United States would spend $50 billion through the war, essentially ending the Great Depression.

April 11, 1941   Roosevelt creates the Office of Price Administration and Civilian Supply (OPACS) to control the prices of goods and corporate profits.

May 1941   Congress creates the Office of Scientific Research and Development (OSRD) to coordinate technological research.

May 1941   The singing group known as the Andrews Sisters performs at March Field near Los Angeles, California, for those preparing America for war, thus beginning a longstanding tradition for the group throughout the war, including participation in war bond drives.

May 20, 1941   President Roosevelt creates the Office of Civilian Defense (OCD) to help communities prepare for war, and appoints Fiorello La Guardia its director.

May 27, 1941   Roosevelt issues an unlimited national emergency declaration in response to continued Japanese expansion in Southeast Asia; the U.S. begins economic restrictions against Japan.

May 28, 1941   President Roosevelt designates Harold Ickes as the Petroleum Coordinator for National Defense.

June 1941   First Lady Eleanor Roosevelt begins writing a monthly question and answer column "If You Ask Me" for *Ladies' Home Journal* until the spring of 1949 and for *McCall's* from 1949 until her death in 1962.

June 22, 1941 Germany invades the Soviet Union, drawing the Soviets into World War II; Roosevelt extends the Lend-Lease program to the Soviets.

June 25, 1941 Under pressure from A. Philip Randolph and other black American leaders, Roosevelt signs an executive order calling for an end to racial discrimination in hiring practices by war industries.

August 14, 1941 Roosevelt and British leader Winston Churchill sign the Atlantic Charter, spelling out their goals in the war.

August 28, 1941 Roosevelt creates the Supplies Priorities and Allocations Board (SPAB) to guide OPM in war mobilization.

September 1941 Eleanor Roosevelt is appointed assistant national director for the Office of Civilian Defense (OCD), the first government position ever held by a First Lady in U.S. history.

September 27, 1941 Henry Kaiser's shipyards complete the first Liberty Ship, over a thousand more of such cargo ships would follow.

December 1941 Shortly after the bombing of Pearl Harbor, actress Dorothy Lamour volunteers her services to sell war bonds to the public to help finance the war; traveling to war plants, among other places, Lamour sold some $300 million of the bonds.

December 1, 1941 The Civil Air Patrol is established to patrol the nation's borders and coastal areas by air.

December 7, 1941 Japan launches a surprise air attack on U.S. military installations at Pearl Harbor, Hawaii, drawing the United States into World War II; the United States declares war on Japan; the following day Germany and Italy declare war on the United States.

December 12, 1941 Five days after the devastating Japanese attacks at Pearl Harbor, Hollywood movie director Frank Capra joins the Signal Corps with a major's commission to devote his filmmaking talent to improving Army morale with war documentaries.

1942 Congress establishes the Emergency Farm Labor Program.

1942 Esther Bubley begins her documentary photography work for the U.S. Office of War Information (OWI).

1942 The War Labor Board (WLB) is created to control wages.

January 1942 German submarines become more prevalent off the U.S. East Coast.

January 2, 1942 Japanese forces capture the capital city of the Philippines as American forces begin a retreat to the Bataan Peninsula.

January 16, 1942 Roosevelt creates the War Production Board (WPB), headed by Donald Nelson, to oversee mobilization and determine which consumer goods should be discontinued or limited in production and to set war production goals.

January 30, 1942 Congress passes the Emergency Price Control Act creating the Office of Price Administration (OPA), which has greater authority to control prices.

February 1942 A Japanese submarine briefly shells a coastal oil field near Santa Barbara, California; President Roosevelt establishes the Volunteer Port Security Force to protect ports and waterfront facilities.

February 7, 1942 The Pittsburgh *Courier,* a prominent black American newspaper, introduces the Double V campaign representing victory over the enemies abroad and victory over racial prejudice on the home front.

February 10, 1942 The WPB bans production of civilian automobiles, paving the way for conversion of the Michigan auto industry to production of warplanes, tanks, military trucks, and other military equipment.

February 19, 1942 Roosevelt signs Executive Order 9066 authorizing removal of Japanese aliens and Japanese Americans to detention centers.

March 21, 1942 The evacuation of Japanese Americans and Japanese aliens to internment camps begins.

April 1942 Roosevelt creates the War Manpower Commission (WMC) to direct workers to more critical industries and areas of workforce shortages.

April 6, 1942 By this date some six million citizens had planted victory gardens, leading to a major contribution to the nation's food supply.

April 26, 1942 Mine Okubo reports to a central relocation station to receive instructions on evacuation to a Japanese American relocation camp.

April 28, 1942 OPA issues the General Maximum Price Regulation, known as General Max, setting price controls.

May 1942 Food rationing begins; War Ration Book One is issued, with sugar being the first table food rationed.

May 1942 The United States and Mexico reach agreement on the *bracero* program, which allows some one hundred thousand Mexican citizens to enter the United States to help solve the farm labor shortage.

May 8, 1942 In an early key military victory in the Pacific, the U.S. defeats a Japanese fleet in the Battle of the Coral Sea.

May 14, 1942 Congress creates the Women's Army Auxiliary Corp (WAAC) with Oveta Culp Hobby its director; some 150,000 would serve.

June 7, 1942 In another major U.S. victory in the Pacific, the U.S. Navy defeats the Japanese fleet in the Battle of Midway.

June 13, 1942 Roosevelt creates the Office of War Information (OWI), with Elmer Davis as its head, to coordinate release of war information to the public.

July 16, 1942 The National War Labor Board (NWLB) establishes the "Little Steel Formula" to control wage increases.

July 30, 1942 Roosevelt signs a bill authorizing women to be accepted into the U.S. Navy, Coast Guard, and U.S. Marines, including the navy's Women Accepted for Volunteer Emergency Service (WAVES) in which 90,000 would serve.

August 7, 1942 U.S. forces begin the offensive in the Pacific with the invasion of Guadalcanal in the Solomon Islands.

September 1942 The first Hollywood World War II combat movie is released titled *Wake Island*.

September 1942 Pilot Nancy Love becomes director of the newly created Women's Auxiliary Ferry Squadron (WAFS), which is charged with ferrying military aircraft to their destinations for service.

September 9, 1942 A lone Japanese float plane, launched from a submarine, drops incendiary bombs in a remote forest area of southwest Oregon causing little damage.

September 10, 1942 The U.S. Army creates the Women's Auxiliary Ferry Squadron (WAFS) to fly planes to needed destinations.

October 3, 1942 The Hollywood Canteen opens with Hollywood actresses Bette Davis giving the opening speech and Betty Grable performing and joining other stars in dancing with the young servicemen before they depart for overseas.

October 3, 1942 Congress passes the Economic Stabilization Act creating the Office of Economic Stabilization (OES), headed by James F. Byrnes, to control the economy and guide the complex rationing program.

October 21, 1942 Congress passes the Revenue Act, restructuring the U.S. income tax system to help finance the war.

November 8, 1942 Allied forces launch a major military offensive in North Africa against German forces.

November 23, 1942 The Coast Guard creates their women's reserves, known as SPAR.

November 29, 1942 Coffee is rationed.

December 1, 1942 A complex system of gasoline rationing begins.

December 2, 1942 President Roosevelt establishes the Petroleum Administration for War with Harold Ickes as its lead.

1943 Over 3.5 million American Red Cross volunteers repair military clothing, wrap bandages, and put together care packages for servicemen overseas.

1943 Maya Angelou becomes the first black American conductor of cable cars on the streets of San Francisco, California.

1943 Actress Betty Grable becomes the number one female star as well as the favorite pin-up girl of military servicemen.

January 12, 1943 Roosevelt declares this date Farm Mobilization Day, claiming food was also a weapon in the war.

January 15, 1943 The Pentagon building is dedicated in the Washington, D.C., area to house the War Department; construction had started in September 1941.

January 31, 1943 Russian troops defeat German forces at Stalingrad marking the first major defeat of Germany and a turning point in the war.

February 1943 Congress establishes a national farm policy for solving farm labor shortages with such programs as the Women's Land Army (WLA) and the Victory Farm Volunteers (VFV).

February 1943 Roosevelt signs an order expanding normal workweeks from 40 to 48 hours.

February 1943 War Ration Book Two is issued as canned goods, dried beans, and peas come under rationing; shoe rationing also begins to conserve the use of leather.

February 13, 1943 U.S. Marine Corps adds the Women's Reserve; 23,000 women joined.

March 29, 1943 The rationing of meat begins.

April 1943 Home economist Florence Louise Hall is appointed chief of the Women's Land Army (WLA), with the goal to recruit and organize large numbers of women to provide farm labor. In all some 1.5 million non-farm women entered the farm labor force.

May 28, 1943 Roosevelt creates the Office of War Mobilization (OWM) to resolve disputes over workforce and raw material shortages.

June 1943 Congress passes the Bolton Act establishing the Cadet Nurse Corps program to recruit and train nurses for wartime duty; 59,000 would serve in the Army Nurse Corps and 11,000 in the Navy Nurse Corps.

June 1943 A series of violent racial conflicts erupts in the United States, including one in Detroit, Michigan, and the "Zoot Suit Riot" in Los Angeles, California.

June 1943 Congress passes the Smith-Connolly War Labor Disputes Act that gives the government power to seize and operate plants where workers are on strike.

July 1943 War mobilization is complete, as industry is able to meet ongoing military needs through the remainder of the war.

July 1, 1943 Oveta Hobby becomes the first female commanding officer in the U.S. Army as the WAAC is given full military status and renamed the Women's Army Corps (WAC), making it part of the regular U.S. Army.

July 10, 1943 Following victory in North Africa, Allied forces invade Sicily, a large island south of Italy, and then Italy itself on September 3.

July 25, 1943 The Women's Aircraft Service Program (WASP) is formed from the WAFS and other organizations; it is ended December 20, 1944.

September 8, 1943 Italy surrenders to Allied forces.

November 28, 1943 Roosevelt, Churchill, and Joseph Stalin, premier of the Soviet Union, convene a three day meeting at Tehran, Iran, to discuss war strategies against Germany and Italy.

January 1944 Mine Okubo leaves her relocation camp and moves to New York City to work for *Fortune* magazine, beginning an illustrious art career.

January 10, 1944 Congress passes the Servicemen's Readjustment Act, known as the GI Bill, that provides generous benefits in housing, education, and business loans to U.S. war veterans.

March 7, 1944 The United States reports that women constitute 42 percent of the workers in West Coast aircraft plants.

June 6, 1944 Allied forces launch the largest sea invasion in history, called Operation Overlord, on the shores of Normandy, France.

August-October 1944 An international conference held at Dumbarton Oaks in Washington, D.C., creates the beginning of the United Nations.

August 25, 1944 Paris, France, is liberated from German occupation by Allied forces.

September 13, 1944 Allied ground forces enter Germany.

October 26, 1944 In the largest naval battle in history, known as the Battle of Leyte Gulf, the U.S. Navy largely destroys the Japanese fleet.

November 1944 The WAVES and SPAR are opened to black American women; the WAC has been open to blacks since its beginning.

November 1944 Japanese begin launching balloon bombs, designed to float across the Pacific Ocean and explode in North America, from Japan; nine thousand are launched over the next several months.

November 7, 1944 Roosevelt wins reelection to a fourth term as U.S. president.

December 1944 Roosevelt revamps OWM to the Office of War Mobilization and Reconversion (OWMR) to coordinate change of war industries back to peacetime production.

December 16, 1944 German forces launch a major counterattack against advancing Allied forces, known as the Battle of the Bulge.

1945 Bill Mauldin, creator of the wartime comic strip "Willie and Joe," wins a Pulitzer Prize for editorial cartooning.

February 1, 1945 Soviet forces advance through Poland and into Germany to within one hundred miles of the German capital of Berlin.

February 4, 1945 The Yalta Conference, held in the Crimean region of the Soviet Union, begins and runs for seven days. The three key allied leaders, U.S. President Franklin D. Roosevelt, British Prime Minister Winston Churchill, and Soviet Premier Joseph Stalin, discuss German surrender terms, a Soviet attack against Japanese forces, and the future of Eastern Europe.

April 12, 1945 Roosevelt dies suddenly from a brain hemorrhage; he is replaced by Harry Truman.

April 18, 1945 Noted war correspondent Ernie Pyle is killed by enemy fire near Okinawa, Japan.

April 25, 1945 Fifty nations begin meeting in San Francisco, California, to write the United Nations (UN) charter.

April 28, 1945 Italian dictator Benito Mussolini is captured and executed by Italian resistance fighters.

April 30, 1945 German dictator Adolf Hitler commits suicide in a fortified bunker beneath Berlin.

May 1945   Six people are killed in southern Oregon by a Japanese balloon bomb.

May 7, 1945   Germany surrenders to allied forces leaving Germany and its capital of Berlin divided into four military occupation zones with American, British, French, and Soviet forces; Americans celebrate the following day, known as V-E Day (Victory in Europe Day).

June 21, 1945   Japanese forces are essentially defeated in major fighting for over two months on the island of Okinawa.

June 26, 1945   Fifty nations meeting in San Francisco, California, sign the United Nations charter.

July 16, 1945   Elda Anderson and other scientists witness the first successful test of the atomic bomb in the New Mexico desert.

July 26, 1945   U.S. president Harry S. Truman, Stalin, and Churchill meet at Potsdam to discuss postwar conditions of Germany.

August 6, 1945   The United States drops an atomic bomb on Hiroshima, Japan, followed by a second bomb on August 9 on Nagasaki.

August 14, 1945   Japan surrenders, ending World War II. Americans celebrate the following day, known as V-J Day (Victory over Japan Day).

September 2, 1945   Formal surrender papers are signed by Japan aboard a U.S. warship in Tokyo Bay.

1946   Artist Mine Okubo publishes a book about Japanese American internment during World War II titled *Citizen 13660,* providing one of the first inside descriptions of the internment experience.

July 1946   Pilot Nancy Love and her husband become the first couple in U.S. history to be decorated at the same time for their military service, with Nancy receiving the Air Medal for her pioneering work.

June 12, 1948   Congress makes the Women's Army Corp (WAC) a permanent part of the U.S. Army.

1988   The U.S. government issues a formal apology to Japanese Americans for their treatment during World War II on the home front.

1997 The Franklin D. Roosevelt Memorial is dedicated in Washington, D.C., commemorating his leadership through the Great Depression and World War II.

June 29, 2001 A national monument is dedicated in Washington, D.C., in the memory of Japanese Americans in World War II.

May 2004 The World War II Memorial is dedicated in Washington, D.C. The memorial honors not only those who fought in the war, but commemorates the great efforts and sacrifices made by those on the American home front as well.

Words to Know

A

aliens: Immigrants who hold citizenship in a foreign country.

Allies: Over thirty nations, including the United States, Great Britain, and Soviet Union, who united in the fight against Germany, Italy, and Japan during World War II.

appeasement: Giving in to the demands of another nation in order to maintain peace.

atomic bomb: A bomb whose massive explosive force comes from the nuclear fission of uranium or plutonium.

Authoritarian: A political system in which authority is centered in a ruling party that demands complete obedience of its citizens and is not legally accountable to the people.

auxiliary: Volunteers who provide additional or supplementary assistance, or an organization that is supplemental to a larger one, such as the auxiliary police or firemen.

Axis powers: Nations who fought against the Allies in World War II including Germany, Italy, and Japan.

B

baby boomers: The population of 76 million children born after World War II, between 1946 and 1964.

barrage balloons: A network of balloons, steel cables, and nets placed over a town or city to protect against attacking enemy aircraft.

bereavement: Grieving over the death of a loved one.

black market: Illegally selling goods in violation of government regulations, such as selling rationed items at very high prices.

blackouts: Completely concealing or turning off all lights from outside view to guard against air raids.

Braceros: Mexican workers recruited by the United States to fill wartime labor shortages, particularly in the area of farm labor.

C

canteen: A place where food, rest, and entertainment are available, usually operated by volunteers.

capital: Money and property.

capitalism: An economic system in which private business and markets, largely free of government intervention, determine the prices, distribution, and production of goods.

cash and carry: The program established in late 1939 by the United States to sell war materials to Great Britain, but Britain had to transport them in their own ships.

civil defense: Non-military programs designed to protect U.S. citizens from enemy attack or disasters on the home front.

civil liberties: Protection of certain basic rights from government interference, such as freedom of speech and religion.

coalition: A temporary alliance of different groups.

Cold War: A prolonged conflict for world dominance from 1945 to 1991 between the two superpowers, the democratic, capitalist United States and the communist Soviet Union. The weapons of conflict were commonly words of propaganda and threats, not military conflicts.

commodity: An economic good produced by industry.

communism: A political and economic system where a single party controls all aspects of citizens' lives and private ownership of property is banned.

conservatism: Opposition to a large federal government and extensive social programs.

D

deficit spending: A government spending more money than the revenue coming in.

democracy: A system of government, such as that of the United States, that allows multiple political parties. Their members are elected to various government offices by popular vote of the people.

dictatorship: A form of government in which one person wields absolute power and control over the people.

dimouts: To turn out some lights, such as along a coastal shore area, particularly those lights pointed toward or easily seen from the ocean to guard against attacks from the sea.

draft: A legal requirement that young men serve in the military for their country for certain periods of time; also more formally known as selective service system.

E

espionage: Using spies to acquire information about the activities of a foreign nation.

F

fascism: A political system in which a strong central government, usually run by a dictator, controls the nation, gaining support through promotion of strong nationalism and often racism; promotes the good of the state above individual rights.

furlough: A brief leave of absence from duty granted to a soldier.

G

G.I.: Nickname for military servicemen derived from the term "government issue."

G.I. Bill: Formally known as the Servicemen's Readjustment Act of 1944; provided extensive economic benefits to World War II veterans, including school expenses and low interest loans for buying homes and starting businesses and farms.

Great Depression: A major economic crisis lasting from 1929 to 1941 leading to massive unemployment and widespread hunger in the U.S. and abroad.

Gross National Product (GNP): The total value of goods and services produced in a country for a particular period of time, such as annually.

I

incendiary bombs: Two- to ten-pound bombs designed to start fires.

incentives: Providing a reward to cause people to take specific actions, such as industries promised certain levels of profits to switch from production of consumer goods to war materials.

induction: A civilian enrolling into the military.

internment camps: A series of ten guarded camps mostly in the western United States where a total of 112,000 Japanese Americans and Japanese aliens were detained during the war for fear of sabotage or espionage. Also known as relocation camps.

isolationism: Opposition to foreign commitments or involvement in foreign disputes.

Issei: Japanese immigrants to the United States.

J

Jim Crow: Jim Crow laws enforced legal segregation, keeping races separated in every aspect of life from schools to restrooms and water fountains; particularly common in the South.

L

Lend-Lease: A U.S. program to supply war materials to foreign countries with payment to be delayed until after the war.

liberal: Those who look to social improvement through government action, such as providing financial security and healthcare not traditionally provided by the national government.

M

market: The world of commerce operating relatively free of government interventions, where demand and availability of goods and materials determines prices, distribution, and production levels.

mass production: To produce in large quantities in an assembly line fashion with the process broken down into many small steps.

mechanization: To replace human or animal labor with machines, such as tanks and trucks.

merchant marines: Officers and crews of U.S. vessels that engage in commerce.

migrant: A person who travels from place to place, often searching for work.

military-industrial complex: A politically powerful alliance of the military services and industry that provides materials to the military.

mobilization: To transform the national economy from peacetime production of goods and foods to wartime production.

munitions: Various types of ammunition such as guns, grenades, and bombs.

N

nationalism: Holding a strong loyalty to one's country and seeking or maintaining independence from other nations.

Nazi: A political party in Germany, more formally known as the National Socialist German Worker's Party, led by Adolf Hitler from 1920 to 1945.

New Deal: The 1930s programs designed by President Franklin D. Roosevelt to promote economic recovery from the Great Depression.

O

organized labor: A collective effort by workers and labor organizations to seek better working conditions.

P

patriotism: Love or devotion to one's country.

prefabricated: To build the parts in separate locations and assemble them at another site, such as a ship or a house.

propaganda: Information aimed at shaping opinions of people, usually by a government.

R

racism: To be prejudiced against people of another race.

rationing: A government system to limit the amount of certain foods and other items in short supply that could be sold to citizens to conserve materials.

riveter: One who fastens metal pieces together, such as airplane or ship parts, with flattened metal bolts.

Rosie the Riveter: A fictional female character appearing on posters and in advertisements recruiting women to work in the war industries.

S

sabotage: To destroy military or industrial facilities.

scrap drives: A public program of gathering discarded or unused items made of materials needed by the defense industry, such as rubber tires, metal pots and pans, and nylon hose.

segregation: To keep races separate, such as in public places and the U.S. military during World War II.

Social Security: A federal program that provides economic assistance for citizens including the aged, retired, unemployed, and disabled.

socialism: An economic and political system in which the government controls all means of production.

strike: A work stoppage to force an employer to meet worker demands.

subversive: People working secretly to overthrow a government.

T

theater of war: Specific regions of the world where World War II was fought, such as the European theater or the Pacific theater.

totalitarian states: Countries where every aspect of life is tightly controlled by a dictator and all citizens must conform.

V

V-E Day: The day victory in Europe was celebrated, May 8, 1945.

victory gardens: Small fruit and vegetable gardens grown by individuals or families, planted in their own yards and public places, such as parks, to supplement the commercial production of food.

V-J Day: The day victory over Japan was celebrated, August 15, 1945.

V-mail: Personal letters written to servicemen overseas on special forms that were photographed onto microfilm, transported to their destination, then printed on paper and delivered to the addressee; designed to conserve cargo space.

W

war bonds: Government certificates sold to individuals and corporations to raise money to finance the war, with the purchaser receiving their money back plus interest at a future time.

wildcat strikes: Worker strikes that do not have the support of organized labor unions.

American Home Front in World War II
Biographies

Elda Anderson

Born October 5, 1899
Green Lake, Wisconsin
Died April 17, 1961
Oak Ridge, Tennessee

Physicist

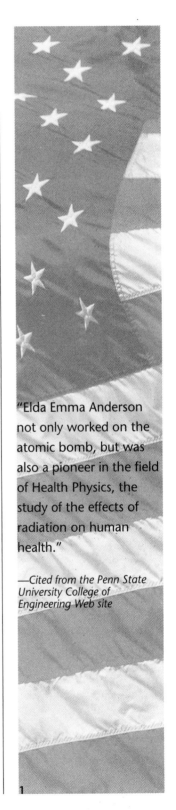

E lda Anderson was a member of the U.S. team of scientists who developed the atomic bomb during World War II (1939–45). She was a physicist with the Manhattan Project and was present at the Trinity Event, which was the first atomic explosion that took place in the New Mexico desert in 1945.

Following the war Anderson became an internationally recognized authority on radiation protection and health physics. In 1955 she was a founding member of the Health Physics Society that sought independent status for the new science. In 1960 she helped formally establish the American Board of Health Physics, a professional certifying agency. Anderson was the first person to serve as chief of education and training in the Health Physics Division of the Oak Ridge National Laboratory in Oak Ridge, Tennessee. She published a *Manual of Radiological Protection for Civil Defense,* and was named a fellow of the American Association for the Advancement of Science.

"Elda Emma Anderson not only worked on the atomic bomb, but was also a pioneer in the field of Health Physics, the study of the effects of radiation on human health."

—*Cited from the Penn State University College of Engineering Web site*

Emily Dunning Barringer

Like Dr. Elda Anderson, Dr. Emily Dunning Barringer (1876–1961) was a woman of science who would prove to have a major impact on World War II (1939–45). Barringer attended Cornell University and Women's Medical School in New York City, graduating in 1901. She ultimately received an appointment to the staff of New York's Gouverneur Hospital to complete her internship and residency (on-the-job training required to complete one's medical education). The public announcement made headline news as she was the first woman in America to be given such an opportunity.

Barringer's initial application to the hospital had been refused because she was a woman. Acceptable employment for women outside of the home at the end of the nineteenth century included teaching, dressmaking, and even nursing, but in the world of medicine, female physicians were struggling to establish their place. The general municipal hospitals of New York City and the large private hospitals held to the tradition of not recommending qualified women physicians for the staff of general medical and surgical services. This denied them residency, or internship, which was required in order for the woman physician to have equal opportunity with the male physicians in all hospital training before entering private practice.

Once Barringer was accepted as a regular intern in the hospital from 1902 to 1904, part of her training included riding the horse-drawn ambulance on emergency calls in the city. She was the first and only woman ambulance surgeon in the world at the time. In 1905 Barringer became the first woman to serve as house surgeon in a New York

A scientist's journey

Elda Emma Anderson was born on October 5, 1899, in the small Wisconsin town of Green Lake, the second of three children of Edwin A. and Lena Heller Anderson. Elda enjoyed math and science as a child and aspired to be a kindergarten teacher but ultimately set her ambitions on a career in science. Her early display of intellectual ability showed promise to her family, and they fully supported her academic plans. It was very uncommon for women to attend college in those days.

Elda Anderson graduated from high school in Green Lake and then attended nearby Ripon College, earning her undergraduate degree in 1922. She obtained a graduate assistantship in physics from the University of Wisconsin and

City hospital. She campaigned for women's access to medical education and, by her example, she secured the opening of general city hospitals in New York City to women.

During World War I (1914–18) the American Women's Hospitals (AWH) War Service Committee was staging a financial drive in order to allow women's participation in the war effort. Barringer was vice chairman of the AWH at the time and one day she rode her ambulance up and down Wall Street (the financial center of New York City) raising money to finance women physicians on their way to devastated France and Serbia in Europe. Barringer would ultimately practice medicine for fifty years, including clinical work in Vienna, Austria.

During World War II the comptroller general of the United States ruled that the law permitting the president to commission qualified persons for service in the U.S. Army did not apply to women physicians. Barringer was called on to chair a special commission of the American Medical Women's Association to change the law. The commission asserted that when judged solely on merit, women perform equally as well as men. The group was successful in its lobbying for legislation to allow female medical doctors to secure commissions in the U.S. Army and Navy. Bill H.R. 1857, called The Sparkman Act, was "An act to provide for the appointment of female physicians and surgeons in the Medical Corps of the Army and Navy." President Franklin D. Roosevelt (1882–1945; served 1933–45) signed the bill on April 16, 1943. For the first time the United States went on record as commissioning women physicians in time of war.

earned her master's degree from the institution in 1924. Anderson went on to teach in local colleges and high schools before joining the physics department at Milwaukee-Downer College, where she became chairman of the department in 1934. She continued working on her doctoral degree, which she received from Wisconsin in 1941.

The atomic bomb

In 1941 Anderson's career took a dramatic turn. She requested a sabbatical leave from teaching and became a staff member in the Office of Scientific Research and Development at Princeton University in New Jersey. Soon after the United

States entered World War II in December 1941, President **Franklin D. Roosevelt** (1882–1945; served 1933–45) learned that the Germans were working on developing an atomic bomb. (European and U.S. scientists had been working on developing the fission process of splitting the uranium atoms for energy in the 1930s, and thought of its use on atomic bombs arose in 1939.) He immediately established an American atomic research program called the Manhattan Project. The main laboratory was set up in the secluded community of Los Alamos, New Mexico, in order for the scientists to be able to work more closely together and in secret. Anderson's work at Princeton led her to become a member of the Manhattan Project in 1943, as the department she was working at became the Manhattan Engineering District. She moved to the Los Alamos Scientific Laboratory in New Mexico, where she joined other scientists working to develop an atomic bomb. There was great pressure to ensure that the United States developed the bomb before Germany. The hectic pace at Los Alamos often demanded eighteen-hour days.

Anderson was part of the cyclotron group that used an accelerator to propel particles such as ions and protons at very high speeds. Her research focused on spectroscopy, the physics that deals with interactions between matter and radiation. This research was vital to the construction of the atomic bomb and also of use in nuclear reactor design. (Nuclear reactors are devices in which a nuclear reaction is started—and controlled—thus producing heat, which is usually used to generate electricity.) The group of physicists completed its construction in the summer of 1945 and took the bomb to the Alamogordo Bombing Range in the New Mexico desert. Their work culminated in what was called the Trinity Event, the explosion of the first atomic bomb on July 16.

There was great excitement among the scientists at their accomplishment and yet great anxiety about what it meant for the future. Germany had already surrendered by this time, and Japan became the ultimate target for the use of two atomic bombs as military weapons in August 1945, killing 150,000 Japanese citizens. In reaction to this experience, Anderson left Los Alamos, New Mexico, in 1947, determined to work toward protecting people and the environment from the harmful effects of radiation.

A new beginning

After her work in Los Alamos, Anderson returned to Milwaukee-Downer College to resume her chairmanship of the physics department. In 1949 she moved to Oak Ridge, Tennessee, to become the first chief of education and training in the Health Physics Division of the Oak Ridge National Laboratory. Her extensive physics background and pioneering spirit led her to explore the new field of health physics, which was the study of the effects of radiation on human health. Anderson was both mentor and friend to the graduate students she taught at Oak Ridge. She encouraged them to expand the science, and they were her legacy to ensure the work would go on. Anderson also worked with faculty members at Vanderbilt University in Nashville, Tennessee, to create a master's degree program in health physics at their institution. She organized international courses in her field in Stockholm, Sweden, in 1955, followed by Belgium in 1957 and Bombay, India, in 1958.

The first nuclear bomb ever developed, prior to its explosion over the New Mexico desert in the Trinity Event in July of 1945. Elda Anderson's work with the other Manhattan Project physicists during World War II led to the U.S. developing the first bomb of its type. *© Corbis. Reproduced by permission.*

Anderson worked throughout her life to promote health physics as a profession. Much of her early work was later used for peaceful applications such as the construction of nuclear reactors. Stricken with leukemia in 1956, Anderson also developed breast cancer in 1961 and died in April of that year. The Elda E. Anderson Award is given annually in her honor to an outstanding individual in the field of health physics.

For More Information

Books

Barringer, Emily Dunning. *Bowery to Bellevue: The Story of New York's First Woman Ambulance Surgeon.* New York: W.W. Norton & Company, 1950.

Parry, Melanie, ed. *Larousse Dictionary of Women.* New York: Larousse, 1996.

Read, Phyllis J., and Bernard L. Witlieb. *The Book of Women's Firsts.* New York: Random House, 1992.

Sicherman, Barbara, and Carol Hurd Green, eds. *Notable American Women: The Modern Period.* Cambridge, MA: Belknap Press, 1980.

Web sites

"Changing the Face of Medicine: Dr. Emily Dunning Barringer." *U.S. National Library of Medicine, National Institutes of Health.* http://www.nlm.nih.gov/changingthefaceofmedicine/physicians/biography_23.html (accessed on June 30, 2004).

"Great American Women: Elda Emma Anderson." *Engineering Projects in Community Service, Purdue University.* http://epics.ecn.purdue.edu/iwt/pciki/GAW/Wisconsin.html (accessed on June 30, 2004).

"Women in Science and Technology: Elda Emma Anderson." *College of Engineering, Penn State University.* http://www.engr.psu.edu/wep/EngCompSp98/AFischer/Elda.html (accessed on June 30, 2004).

The Andrews Sisters

LaVerne Andrews
Born July 6, 1911
Minneapolis, Minnesota
Died May 8, 1967
Brentwood, California

Maxene Andrews
Born January 3, 1916
Minneapolis, Minnesota
Died October 21, 1995
Cape Cod, Massachusetts

Patricia (Patty) Andrews
Born February 16, 1918
Minneapolis, Minnesota

Entertainers

During World War II (1939–45), a trio of sisters known as the Andrews Sisters topped the music charts with hits such as their Oscar-nominated "Boogie-Woogie Bugle Boy." Their names were LaVerne, Maxene, and Patty Andrews, and they were the best-selling female vocal group in the twentieth century.

Touring America for fifty weeks a year, the Andrews Sisters exuded an enthusiasm and positive national spirit that drew Americans together during a dark time. For those serving abroad, the music brought a sense of the familiar and provided a reminder of what they had left behind. The Andrews Sisters sang a wide variety of musical styles that were both patriotic and upbeat while entertaining with the United Services Organization (USO). The trio performed at military posts and hospital wards, for Armed Forces Radio, and at war bond rallies. Although they placed 113 songs on the *Billboard* "Top 40" charts in fifteen years, their singing act will always be associated with World War II.

"He was a famous trumpet man from out Chicago way/ He had a boogie sound that no one else could play/ He was the top man at his craft/ But then his number came up and he was gone with the draft/He's the boogie-woogie bugle boy of Company B."

—*Lyrics from "Boogie-Woogie Bugle Boy"*

From left: Patty, Maxene, and LaVerne Andrews.
AP/Wide World Photos. Reproduced by permission.

The girls next door

LaVerne, Maxene, and Patty Andrews were born in Minneapolis, Minnesota, to Olga Sollie and Peter Andrews. Peter had changed his surname from Andreos to Andrews upon his arrival in America from his homeland in Greece. LaVerne Sophie was born to the couple on July 6, 1911, followed by Maxene Angelyn on January 3, 1916, and Patricia (Patty) Marie on February 16, 1918. They were all exceptional singers and began mimicking radio tunes at an early age. Patty provided a strong lead, Maxene sang soprano (high singing voice), and LaVerne took the alto (low singing voice) part for a smooth blending of their voices in perfect, three-part harmony. The sisters began singing locally and soon received their first professional contract to sing in vaudeville and radio. When the trio started to travel, their parents chaperoned them across America in the family car.

The Andrews Sisters signed a contract with Decca Records in 1937 and had their first number one hit. Its title was "Bei Mir Bist Du Schon," meaning "By Me You Are Beautiful." It was a novelty tune showcasing their ability to vocalize the popular Big Band sound of the era. It went to the number one spot on the radio program *Your Hit Parade*. More hit songs followed. The trio went on to reintroduce a very old style of music from the Deep South, called boogie-woogie.

The Big Band era was now in full swing and the sisters found themselves working nonstop. They had loud and fast harmony, synchronized choreography, and showmanship so perfected that it seemed effortless. However, in reality, it came from four hours of rehearsing each day. The sisters worked with nearly every famous bandleader of the day and covered all styles of music that characterized the 1940s, from be-bop to polkas and swing to waltzes. The Andrews Sisters made their first film appearance in *Argentine Nights* in 1940. They would appear in over a dozen more films throughout the decade. Patty, Maxene, and LaVerne enjoyed a long and successful collaboration with famous singer Bing Crosby (1903–1977) in both film and song.

Morale boosters

In 1941 war clouds were growing darker as Adolf Hitler's (1889–1945) German army conquered most of Europe.

The Big Bands

Like many Hollywood films of the early 1940s, music provided an escape for the American public. Throughout the nation youth crowded dance halls and nightclubs to do dances called the jitterbug and the lindy. Bandleaders were in abundance and became music industry superstars. The list of the most famous always included Jimmy Dorsey (1904–1957). He formed the Jimmy Dorsey Orchestra in 1935 and kept up its high standards. By the end of World War II (1939–45), it had surpassed most other bands in both popularity and in musicianship.

The Big Bands provided an important morale boost to Americans across the home front and especially to those in uniform. The war gave meteoric fame to the bands but many soon found their members swallowed up by enlistment or by the draft. The enlistment of some top stars began as early as the summer of 1942, and many bands floundered at home. New bands began forming in the army by such legendary greats as Glenn Miller (1904–1944).

The manpower shortage being felt across America touched all businesses, and the entertainment business was not immune. Jimmy Dorsey and his orchestra felt the shortages in other areas as well. They needed government "priority" papers saying their trip was essential for the war effort in order to ride a train. Gasoline was rationed, even if they happened to have an automobile, and flying was not an option. Getting an orchestra to its next performance proved a challenge. Some performers were losing work because they were not allowed to travel. By order of their local draft boards, they had to stay in their hometowns to be on hand for an immediate call to military duty. Despite the hardships, Dorsey continued his work of entertaining both troops and civilians while keeping morale high for his own musicians.

Americans remained deeply divided about their role in the European war; most preferring that the United States remain out of it. When Japan attacked Pearl Harbor, Hawaii, on December 7, 1941, the United States officially entered World War II and the nation quickly transformed from the lean years of the Great Depression (the severe economic crisis that lasted from 1929–41) to full-scale military production. On the home front there came rationing of precious goods, air raid drills, blackouts in cities, and war bond drives.

Everyone searched for ways they could contribute to the war effort. Even before Pearl Harbor, the entertainment industry had joined with the United Service Organization (USO; a nonprofit, private organization, totally funded by gifts from citizens and businesses, that worked closely with the military to look after the welfare, spirits, and recreational needs of America's military personnel) in the effort to sustain the morale of America's service men and women as the military rapidly grew in 1940 and 1941. The USO, placed under the general direction of the army and the navy, was financed by the American people through voluntary contributions. In May 1941 a comedian named Bob Hope (1903–2003) took the cast of his weekly radio show to March Field outside Los Angeles, California, to entertain those Americans preparing for war; and so began a longstanding tradition.

The Andrews Sisters found that even though they had been busy enough with three daily shows in the prewar times, they were now being booked for twice that number. Looking for a way to contribute to the war effort, they began visiting camps and hospital wards in every city where they played. They also could be found singing at the Hollywood Canteen, one of the entertainment clubs established for soldiers on leave. Patty, Maxene, and LaVerne performed for the military at every opportunity both at home and abroad, volunteering their services in order to boost morale among those in uniform.

The military encouraged the performers' contribution as it helped ward off the boredom and loneliness that were major problems in the camps and wards. Dancers, musicians, sketch artists, jugglers, comedians, actors, and athletes all wanted involvement in the national defense effort through the USO. Abroad, the USO performers could be found touring the temporary tent cities near the front lines of battle, entertaining soldiers as they waited to press the battle forward. They would then follow the units as soon as an area had been secured.

The USO shows were expanding as rapidly as the Allies' victories. At one point the curtain was going up at USO shows throughout the world over seven hundred times every day. The USO Camp Shows operation broke down into several circuits, bringing specialized entertainment to the troops. The Victory Circuit produced full-size plays and full-dress musicals. The Blue Circuit was composed of small, mobile units of

variety acts. The Hospital Circuit consisted of various kinds of performers who toured eighty general hospitals in the United States. The Foxhole Circuit was made up of a variety of entertainers such as Big Bands and Hollywood stars, many with headline acts and famous names.

On the home front

After appearances at the Paramount Theater in New York City, the Andrews Sisters would go over to Times Square between shows and do free shows on a big stage set up in the center of the square. People formed long lines to buy war bonds used to finance the war, and the entertainers would provide music while they waited. The sisters would sing for two or three hours and then hurry back in time for their theater show. They also volunteered for the "Radio Bond Days" shows being produced by the radio networks at the time. The shows promoted everything from conservation of scrap metals to helpful hints on how to use toothpaste sparingly. Top stars also urged listeners to phone in their pledges for the war bond drive.

The Andrews Sisters continued singing for the troops over the radio through Armed Forces Radio Shows (AFRS), teaming up with Bing Crosby and Bob Hope for the first two shows. Special extra-long playing recordings were put together exclusively for the AFRS so that those abroad were able to listen to music from home with a minimum of interruptions. The soldiers took a special liking to the Andrews Sisters' tune "Rum and Coca-Cola," which came out in 1944. The sisters were told that their hit "Shoo-Shoo, Baby" (1943) was one of the tunes whose title wound up on the noses of American warplanes as they flew into battle. When Europe was finally liberated by the Allies, the Andrews Sisters were given the opportunity to entertain the troops with the USO in North Africa, Sicily, and Europe. In John Sforza's book *Swing It!,* Patty Andrews is quoted as saying, "We were such a part of everybody's life in the Second World War. We represented something overseas and at home—a sort of security."

A changing world

Patty, Maxene, and LaVerne recorded songs intended to give the American people a reason to smile during the war. Even those on the home front who were spared the agony of seeing loved ones listed in the local newspaper under the headings of "killed, wounded, or missing in action," were still suffering from the distress that accompanied long years of separation. The Andrews Sisters' tunes were selected to provide the public with an escape from the worries of war, and their popularity soared throughout the 1940s.

The end of the war in 1945 also marked the beginning of the end of the Big Band era. Many servicemen returning home were starting college under the new GI Bill of Rights. Young couples were beginning families. Budgets did not include dance clubs and entertainment. The Andrews Sisters continued performing for several years before deciding to retire as a group in the 1950s. They reunited for a time but went their separate ways after LaVerne's death in 1967. Their talent, versatility, and worldwide exposure would assure the

Andrews Sisters a place in music history, as they had revolutionized and forever changed popular music.

For More Information

Books

Andrews, Maxene, and Bill Gilbert. *Over Here, Over There: The Andrews Sisters and the USO Stars in World War II*. New York: Kensington Publishing Corp., 1993.

Sforza, John. *Swing It!: The Andrews Sisters Story*. Lexington, KY: University Press of Kentucky, 2000.

Simon, George T. *The Big Bands*. New York: Macmillan, 1967.

Terkel, Studs. *The Good War: An Oral History of World War Two*. New York: Pantheon Books, 1984.

Web sites

"The Andrews Sisters." *Bigbands*. http://www.bigbands.net/andrewsbio.htm (accessed on July 18, 2004).

Maya Angelou

Born April 4, 1928
St. Louis, Missouri

Poet, author, actress, director

"Her personal outreach to improve conditions for women in the Third World, primarily in Africa, has helped change the lives of thousands less privileged."

—Cited from the Women's International Center Web site

Maya Angelou.
© Bettmann/Corbis.
Reproduced by permission.

Decades before she rose to great acclaim in the arts, Maya Angelou was breaking down barriers and laying the groundwork for her life's mission of helping others. As a teenager during World War II (1939–45), she became the first black American streetcar conductor in San Francisco, California. She also witnessed firsthand the removal of thousands of Japanese American citizens from San Francisco by the War Relocation Authority (WRA). These citizens were forced to leave their homes and evacuate to camps spread throughout the United States. The tragic scene made a lasting impression on Angelou, who worked to better the lives of others the rest of her life.

Angelou became a noted author, poet, teacher, and historian. The first black American woman director in Hollywood, Angelou wrote, produced, directed, and acted in productions for stage, film, and television. She worked with Dr. Martin Luther King Jr. (1929–1968) and actively participated in the movement for civil rights in America and in South Africa during the 1950s. On January 20, 1993, Angelou read her poem "On the Pulse of Morning" for the inauguration of President Bill Clinton (1946–; served 1993–2001) in Washington, D.C.

She held a lifetime appointment as Reynolds Professor of American Studies at Wake Forest University in Winston-Salem, North Carolina, into the twenty-first century.

Growing up during the Great Depression

Marguerite Annie Johnson (later known as Maya Angelou) was born on April 4, 1928, to Vivian Baxter and Bailey Johnson of St. Louis, Missouri. Her brother, Bailey Johnson Jr., was born the previous year. The family moved west to Long Beach, California, soon after Marguerite's birth. When their parents divorced in 1931, the two youngsters, Marguerite and Bailey, were sent alone on a long train ride eastward to live with their paternal grandmother, Annie Johnson Henderson, in Stamps, Arkansas. The children called her Momma, and she would take care of them off and on throughout their lives.

When Marguerite turned seven years old, she and Bailey reunited with their mother, who was now living in St. Louis. A year later, Marguerite suffered an assault at the hands of one of her mother's boyfriends. The trauma left the little girl without a voice. The children were returned to Momma in Stamps, where Marguerite remained mute for five years, speaking only to her trusted brother Bailey. A local family friend, Bertha Flowers, recognized that Marguerite, despite her muteness, had a literary gift and introduced her to literature. She read to her, showed her the books in her own library, and invited the child to borrow them under one condition: Marguerite must read them out loud. Because she loved to read and loved the personal attention from Mrs. Flowers, Marguerite slowly began to speak again.

In 1940 Marguerite graduated at the top of her eighth grade class from the racially segregated Lafayette County Training School. She said good-bye to her beloved grandmother as she and Bailey left Arkansas to move back into their mother's home, this time in San Francisco, California. At age thirteen Marguerite excelled in her classes at George Washington High School in the city. She won a scholarship for evening classes at the California Labor School, where she studied drama and dance. It was here that she dreamed of becoming a professional dancer.

World War II

Just as the children were settling into their new lives in California, World War II was threatening America. Their mother and her new husband had purchased a fourteen-room home on Post Street in the Fillmore District of San Francisco and had turned it into a boardinghouse. The lodgers who came to stay at the house were a diverse and interesting group that provided a sharp contrast to the quiet life Marguerite had known in rural Arkansas.

The Fillmore area had previously been the center of San Francisco's large population of Japanese immigrants and their descendants. With the outbreak of World War II, thousands of Japanese Americans were interned in prison camps by the federal government, which considered them a security risk now that Japan had become a declared enemy of the United States. Many Asian American families were forced to sell or leave their homes and businesses and go to live in crowded camps because of their ancestral background. Marguerite was witness to a form of racism different from what she had seen in the South. Few people spoke out against the internment but the experience made an impact on Marguerite's life.

In a short time, black Americans replaced the Japanese American population of Fillmore. Many blacks were lured to the city from rural areas by the ready availability of jobs in various industries rejuvenated by the war, such as shipping and munitions manufacturing. For black Americans in urban areas, the war meant a period of relative prosperity. The Fillmore district in San Francisco was a bustling center of activity.

When Marguerite was fifteen years old, she decided to get a job. Many jobs that were usually performed by men were now opened to women because of the war. She noticed women working as streetcar conductors and decided she wanted to be one. At the time, however, blacks were not allowed to work on streetcars. For a month Marguerite arrived every morning at the company office until she was allowed to fill out an application for the job. She added four years to her true age on the application and the company finally hired her. She became the first black American conductor of cable cars on the streets of San Francisco.

Struggling to survive

In 1945 World War II ended and the country was celebrating victory over Germany and Japan. Marguerite received her diploma from Mission High School and several months later gave birth to her son Clyde (Guy) Bailey Johnson. At the age of seventeen she now had a child of her own to raise. She worked a variety of jobs in order to support her son, and even tried to join the army in the late 1940s to receive some vocational training, but she was turned down. Marguerite finally ended up in sales in a record store, where she was able to indulge her love of music. It was there that she met Tosh Angelos, a Greek American soldier who shared her interest in jazz music and adored Guy. Marguerite and Angelos were married in 1952.

Marguerite had studied dance for years. She decided to put her natural talent and years of training to the test by trying to make a living in the entertainment industry. She soon found work in nightclubs and began using the name Rita Johnson until her act brought her to the attention of the owners of the Purple Onion, San Francisco's most popular club at the time. The owners hired her to work for them but decided that she needed a more theatrical name and set about helping her choose one. They settled on Maya, which was her brother Bailey's nickname for her, and the name that her family called her. Her married name Angelos was turned into Angelou and she debuted at the Purple Onion as Maya Angelou in 1953.

Talent scouts saw Angelou perform, and she was chosen to be a member of the all-black cast for the musical *Porgy and Bess,* which was touring Europe and Africa. Angelou stayed with the tour from 1954 to 1955 but missed her son too much and returned to the United States to be with him. Maya and Tosh Angelos divorced in 1954, and Angelou continued making a living as a nightclub singer.

The civil rights movement

In 1959 Maya Angelou took Guy and settled in Brooklyn, New York, where she worked to establish herself as a nightclub singer and actress. She knew she wanted to write so she joined the Harlem Writers' Guild, a group of excellent black American writers. Dr. Martin Luther King Jr. was leading

A Best-Selling Author and Poet

Maya Angelou published many books of verse and stories of her amazing life including her home front experiences as a San Francisco streetcar conductor. In addition to *I Know Why the Caged Bird Sings* (1969), she published other autobiographies, including *Gather Together in My Name* (1974), *The Heart of a Woman* (1981), and *All God's Children Need Traveling Shoes* (1986). Following her highly acclaimed first book of poetry titled *Just Give Me a Cool Drink of Water 'fore I Diiie* in 1971 came many other books of verse and meditation, including *Oh Pray My Wings Are Gonna Fit Me Well* (1975), *Wouldn't Take Nothing For My Journey Now* (1993), *Life Doesn't Frighten Me* (1993), *Even the Stars Look Lonesome* (1997), and *A Song Flung Up to Heaven* (2002). Random House publishers released *The Complete Collected Poems of Maya Angelou* in 1994. In 1999 Maya Angelou received the prestigious Lifetime Achievement Award for Literature.

the civil rights movement seeking racial justice in America at the time. Angelou heard him speak and decided to help raise awareness about the civil rights struggle. She and another performer wrote, produced, and appeared in the revue *Cabaret for Freedom* in order to raise money for the Southern Christian Leadership Conference (SCLC) that King led.

While working as northern coordinator of the SCLC Angelou met and fell in love with South African freedom fighter Vusumzi Make. She and Guy moved with Make to Cairo, Egypt, where Angelou worked as a journalist. In 1963 Angelou took Guy and moved to Accra, Ghana, in West Africa. She continued working as a journalist until returning to the United States in 1965.

National recognition

In the late 1960s Angelou focused her energies on her writing. The first installment of her autobiography, titled *I Know Why the Caged Bird Sings,* was published in 1969. In the book, Angelou describes the hardship of her early years during the Great Depression of the 1930s and the home front war years of the early 1940s. Both humorous and touching, she realistically related the human condition as seen through the eyes of a young black girl from the South. The book became an immediate best-seller and was nominated for a National Book Award.

During the 1970s and 1980s, Angelou wrote and published four more volumes of her autobiography and several books of poetry. In 1972 she was nominated for a Pulitzer prize for her first published book of verse, *Just Give Me a Cool Drink of Water 'fore I Diiie* (1971). She was the first black American woman to attain membership in the Directors Guild, and became the first to have a screenplay produced in Hollywood when she wrote the script for *Georgia, Georgia* (1971). Angelou adapted her first autobiography, *I Know Why the Caged Bird Sings,* for television in 1970 and was later nominated for an Emmy award for her acting performance in the television miniseries *Roots* (1977). She was also nominated for a Tony award for her Broadway debut in *Look Away* (1975).

In 1981 Angelou became a literature professor at Wake Forest University in North Carolina and continued writing. She received numerous honorary degrees and worked as a literacy activist with the goal of helping to eliminate illiteracy. Traveling extensively, Angelou gave readings and spoke to audiences about her writing and about the lessons she learned throughout her life. In 1996 Angelou was appointed as a national ambassador for the United Nations International Children's Emergency Fund (UNICEF), an appointment she held into the twenty-first century.

For More Information

Books

Angelou, Maya. *I Know Why the Caged Bird Sings*. New York: Random House, 1969.

Hansen, Joyce. *Women of Hope: African Americans Who Made a Difference*. New York: Scholastic Press, 1998.

King, Sarah E. *Maya Angelou: Greeting the Morning*. Brookfield, CT: Millbrook Press, 1994.

Shapiro, Miles. *Maya Angelou: Author*. Philadelphia, PA: Chelsea House Publishers, 2000.

Web sites

"Maya Angelou." *The Academy of American Poets.* http://www.poets.org/poets/poets.cfm?prmID=88 (accessed on July 18, 2004).

"Maya Angelou: Greatness Through Literature." *Women's International Center.* http://www.wic.org/bio/mangelou.htm (accessed on July 18, 2004).

Esther Bubley

Born 1921
Phillips, Wisconsin
Died 1998
New York City, New York

Photojournalist

"Put me down with people, and it's just overwhelming."

Esther Bubley.
The Library of Congress.

Esther Bubley was a photojournalist whose body of work serves as a document of American culture in the mid-twentieth century. By the mid-1930s photography was mostly concerned with landscapes, snapshots, and family portraits. However, photography was quickly being discovered as a worthy tool of communication in making serious statements. With her unparalleled technical excellence with a camera, Bubley created a visual scene of American society beginning in the 1940s and enduring for decades.

Bubley's photographic documentation of American life began with her documentary photography work for the U.S. Office of War Information (OWI) in 1942 and 1943 on the home front during World War II (1939–45). It continued on an international scale during the golden age of photojournalism from the 1940s to the 1960s. She captured Americans in very ordinary circumstances, going about their usual routines, in images that are compelling while being realistic and artistic as well. Bubley focused on the human dimension of war mobilization on the home front. Her style recalls a **Norman Rockwell** (1894–1978; see entry) manner of American realism,

21

displaying a genuine interest in humanity. Bubley helped set the stage for future photojournalists of the world.

A world in transition

Born in 1921 in Phillips, Wisconsin, to Russian Jewish immigrants Louie and Ida Bubley, Esther was one of five children. She gained an interest in photography early in her life. After graduating from high school, she studied two years at Superior State Teachers College. Esther then transferred to the Minneapolis School of Design in order to complete its one-year photography program. In 1940, at age nineteen, Esther moved to New York City to pursue her dream of becoming a professional photographer.

Esther Bubley spent a brief time as a freelance photographer for *Vogue* magazine before moving to Washington, D.C. There, jobs for women were becoming plentiful due to America's growing war mobilization efforts for World War II. She was first hired to shoot microfilm for the National Archives. Several months later, she moved over to the Historical Section of the Farm Security Administration (FSA) to work as a lab technician in the darkroom. The FSA was organized to provide loans and resettlement opportunities to farmers impoverished by poor land conditions and the economic effects of the Great Depression (1929–41). The Historical Section of the FSA was assigned to document in photographs the agency's activities. Its job was to enhance the public's perception of federal aid for the destitute under President **Franklin D. Roosevelt**'s (1882–1945; served 1933–45; see entry) New Deal program. New Deal was the name given to President Roosevelt's programs to bring relief, recovery, and reform to the United States, pulling the nation out of the Depression.

The government's message of reform was communicated to the American people through a wide variety of mediums. The FSA photographs illustrated government reports and appeared in exhibits as well as newspapers and magazines. Magazines such as *Life* and *The Saturday Evening Post* had become very popular in America in the 1930s, and Bubley longed to be in their pages. She began taking photographs of subjects around the nation's capital in order to prove her camera skills. Her photography impressed her employer

enough to send her on assignments for the FSA away from the laboratory. Quiet and unobtrusive, she was able to earn the trust of her subjects. She put them at ease in order to create photographs that had cultural as well as artistic interest. Her strength was her ability to capture the essence of the moment while remaining respectful of her subjects.

Bubley was one of an impressive group of photographers working for the FSA under the director, Roy Stryker.

Esther Bubley's photographs of Americans in everyday situations such as this one helped document American life before, during, and after World War II. *© Corbis. Reproduced by permission.*

He insisted that they be well informed about their current topic before heading into the field. He assigned books to read and gave informal lectures to educate his photographers. Even though the photographs were to be spontaneous, the preparation work for the photographer was extensive. Stryker knew what he wanted to see and gave explicit instructions, including shooting scripts for each season and each job a photographer was assigned.

Wartime reality

With America's entry into World War II in December 1941, the FSA photographic unit shifted to the Office of War Information (OWI). Its focus changed to ever more positive images of the country in order to boost morale on the home front. Organized by President Roosevelt on June 13, 1942, the OWI became the office of government information for the entire American war effort. The OWI was charged with providing all information to overseas forces as well as communicating between the government and media on the home front. Its task was primarily educational and its images showed a country in transition from the weighted days of the Great Depression to the frantic pace inspired by the war.

Bubley found ample subject matter to explore on the American home front as the nation mobilized for war. She was drawn to real people in their intimate moments. Her images did not necessarily glorify war but caught both patriotic scenes and the human condition without the added wartime sentimentality. She focused on the human situation as opposed to any kind of propaganda (government information given to sway public beliefs), and in doing so she exposed her audience to an honest assessment of wartime America on the home front. By choosing to focus on ordinary people in extraordinary times, she showed a great compassion for her subjects. Her work reflected aspects of wartime life that were often ignored.

A new era

With the end of war in 1945, the OWI was disbanded and its collection of photographs transferred to the Library of

Dorothea Lange

Like Esther Bubley, Dorothea Lange (1895–1965) was another highly skilled female photographer whose camera would document changes on the American home front during World War II (1939–45). Lange focused especially on workers uprooted by the war. Lange's early work covered displaced farm families and migrant workers during the Great Depression (1929–41), when she worked for the Farm Security Administration (FSA). She captured one image of an exhausted thirty-two-year-old migrant mother, with three of her seven children, waiting at the edge of a worker's camp in Nipomo, California. The photograph, "Migrant Mother," is one of the best-known images to come out of the FSA's 145,000-item photographic collection made between 1935 and 1943. It is also one of the most widely reproduced and exhibited photographs in history.

Three months after Japan attacked Pearl Harbor, Hawaii, in December 1941, Lange was hired by the federal War Relocation Authority (WRA) to photograph the internment of Japanese Americans and resident aliens living in the United States. More than 110,000 people of Japanese descent were moved from their homes along the U.S. West Coast into ten wartime camps in remote areas on the American mainland. Lange encountered disturbing racial and civil rights issues raised by the Japanese internment and found herself at odds with her employer, the U.S. government. Executive Order 9066 signed by President Franklin D. Roosevelt (1882–1945; served 1933–45) called for the internment. Many of Lange's photographs showing the indignities suffered by the Japanese internees were censored by the government. The full impact of her photographs was not felt until 1972, when the Whitney Museum included twenty-seven of them in an exhibition titled "Executive Order 9066."

Congress. Bubley put her passion for photography to work in the corporate world, covering the postwar decades throughout the world. She would travel to Europe, Asia, and Australia as well as to Central and South America. In 1954 she became the first female recipient of *Photography* magazine's grand prize in the International Black-and-White division. She earned the award for her photographs of a UNICEF (United Nations International Children's Emergency Fund) medical mission. The mission involved a medical team's treatment of trachoma, an eye disease causing blindness among the desert inhabitants of Morocco.

Bubley became a regular freelance photographer for numerous national magazines. Her best-known work was a celebrated series for *Ladies Home Journal*. The series titled "How America Lives" ran from 1948 through 1960. By the mid-1960s television replaced the popular illustrated magazines as the primary source of news and entertainment, and Bubley retired from her hectic schedule. She settled into her Manhattan, New York, apartment and pursued interests in gardening and animals. Bubley published several books on both of these favored topics. She lived to see a renewed interest in her photography in the 1980s and 1990s. Books and museums continued to showcase her work even after her death in 1998.

For More Information

Books

Lesy, Michael. *Long Time Coming: A Photographic Portrait of America, 1935–1943*. New York: W.W. Norton & Company, 2002.

O'Neill, Lois Decker, ed. *The Women's Book of World Records and Achievements*. Garden City, NY: Anchor Press/Doubleday, 1979.

Parrish, Thomas D., ed. *Encyclopedia of World War II*. New York: Simon and Schuster (A Cord Communications Book imprint), 1978.

Stryker, Roy Emerson, and Nancy Wood. *In This Proud Land: America 1935–1943 As Seen in the FSA Photographs*. Greenwich, CT: New York Graphic Society, 1973.

Web sites

"Dorothea Lange and the Relocation of the Japanese." *Museum of the City of San Francisco*. http://www.sfmuseum.org/hist/lange.html (accessed on July 18, 2004).

"The Photographers: Esther Bubley." *Carnegie Library of Pittsburgh*. http://www.clpgh.org/exhibit/photog6.html (accessed on July 18, 2004).

"Women Come to the Front: Esther Bubley." *Library of Congress*. http://www.loc.gov/exhibits/wcf/wcf0012.html (accessed on July 18, 2004).

Vannevar Bush

Born March 11, 1890
Everett, Massachusetts
Died June 28, 1974
Belmont, Massachusetts

Physicist, electrical research engineer,
inventor, science administrator

A brilliant visionary with his sights always set to the future, engineer and mathematician Vannevar Bush guided much of the rapid-paced scientific research and development of U.S. weapons used to win World War II (1939–45). As a leading scientific advisor to the federal government in the 1940s, he revolutionized the interaction and cooperation between the science community, industry, and government. In doing so, Bush charted a new course in the way science research and its eventual application was carried out in the United States. Additionally, by the start of the twenty-first century, the innovative Bush was widely regarded as the "godfather" of the computer age. By 1945 he had conceptualized a machine he dubbed the "memex" that would follow pathways of stored information to greatly enhance human access to knowledge.

A highly gifted young man

Vannevar Bush was born on March 11, 1890, in Everett, Massachusetts, to Richard Perry Bush and Emma Linwood Paine. Although Vannevar's father was a Universalist

"The anonymous army of U.S. scientists . . . are fighting a deadly, technological war. Their general is a shrewd, imaginative physicist, Dr. Vannevar Bush."

—Time, *April 3, 1944*

Vannevar Bush.
© Bettmann/ Corbis.
Reproduced by permission.

minister, his family tree was peppered with self-confident sea captains accustomed to being in command. Bush attributed his determination to "run the ship" to the influence of his grandfather, a whaling skipper.

Bush was raised in comfortable but modest surroundings in Chelsea, Massachusetts. A stellar student exhibiting considerable talent in math and physics, Bush graduated from Tufts University in 1913 with both a B.S. and M.S. While at Tufts, Bush studied the concepts of electrical engineering that fed his inclination to tinker with scientific ideas until he had invented some practical device. An early invention was a hand-pushed machine that looked like a lawn mower but was a land survey machine that could determine elevations and draw a rough map for the operator. As a young college student, Bush had not yet gathered the people and political skills it would take to effectively market his device. But he learned from experience and by the 1930s and 1940s, Bush would be a master administrator coordinating scientists, and business, military, and government leaders in the development of products to win World War II.

Within one year, 1915, Bush completed a doctorate of engineering program administered through Massachusetts Institute of Technology (MIT) and Harvard. Bush married Phoebe Davis in 1916 and they had two sons. Both boys would serve in the military during World War II—one was an army lieutenant, the other an aviation cadet. That same year, Bush returned to Tufts as an assistant professor. In 1917, eager to aid the World War I (1914–18) effort, he was instrumental in developing an electromagnetic locator to find submarines, only to see it deployed incorrectly and never useful in battle. This experience further pushed Bush to acquire the political and networking skills to assure his intellect and inventions were given due credit.

Scientific theory to practical use

In 1919 Bush joined the electrical engineering department of MIT as an associate professor. By 1923 he was a full professor, and head of both graduate studies and the electrical engineering research department. Continuing his meteoric rise, he soon became vice president of MIT and dean of the college of engineering. During the 1920s and 1930s he invented and built with the help of his students a machine called the differential analyzer, run mechanically by large gears to solve mathematical equations. He also wished to build an automatic machine that would go beyond mathematic equations to store the rapidly expanding information base accumulating at universities. To this end he worked with microfilm as a way to store and retrieve information. Bush's early "computers" would be used extensively before and during World War II to work through many science and engineering problems. In 1934 Bush was elected to the National Academy of Sciences, whose membership comprised the most elite scientists in the United States. During this same time period Bush held an intense interest in working with industry to turn theoretical knowledge into practical application. He concerned himself with patent rights (the exclusive right to manufacture, use, or sell a device) and served on the Science Advisory Board's Committee on the National Relation of the Patent System to the Stimulation of New Industries. Working closely with industry, he helped devise a thermostat whose development ultimately ended up as a basis for the company Texas Instruments. He also developed a gas rectifier (a gaseous tube to convert current for use in radios) so that radios were no longer dependent on batteries. Raytheon Corporation grew from this invention.

In 1937 Bush was well positioned to leave MIT and become president of Carnegie Institution of Washington (CIW). The prestigious CIW was a grouping of well-financed research institutions. At CIW Bush would influence and advise the direction of scientific research in the United States. The war heating up in Europe influenced Bush's thinking on the mobilization of research to aid development of technologies to win the war for the Allied powers (Great Britain, France, and the Soviet Union).

Office of Scientific Research and Development

In 1940 Bush convinced President **Franklin D. Roosevelt** (1882–1945; served 1933–45; see entry) that the United States needed a functioning committee bringing together scientific, industry, military, and government leaders. The committee would coordinate development of war weapons and technologies vital to helping Great Britain and other nations fighting the military expansion of Nazi Germany. (The United States would not enter the war until December 1941, but it was supplying materials and technology to those nations who were already engaged in the fight.) President Roosevelt revived the National Defense Research Committee (NDRC), first conceived in World War I, put Bush in charge, and gave him direct access to the White House and emergency funding. By mid-1941 a new larger agency, the Office of Scientific Research and Development (OSRD), was established and funded by congressional appropriations. The OSRD pulled NDRC, and the new Committee on Medical Research (CMR), under its umbrella. Bush became the OSRD's director, making OSRD completely under civilian control, not under military or governmental control. Bush believed existing government agencies and the military were moving much too slow in research and development. Being highly flexible and able to initiate work rapidly, OSRD began awarding government contracts to the universities and industrial businesses Bush believed were best able to deliver on various projects. Universities receiving contracts included California Institute of Technology (Caltech), University of Chicago, CIW, Columbia University, Harvard University, Johns Hopkins University, and MIT. Companies included Western Electric and Bell Laboratories, General Motors, Westinghouse, Sperry, Philco, Sylvania, Studebaker, Standard Oil, Dupont, and General Electric. Bush arranged for key scientific personnel in the universities, industries, and government to receive draft deferments. Bush's civilian army of top U.S. scientists was approximately six thousand strong. OSRD also worked with essentially all of the army's and navy's research laboratories.

The OSRD limited its scope to the research and development of devices for the military. Bush left project testing, manufacturing, and delivery to the businesses and the military branches. Inevitably, controversies arose over which university and business got what, and between the military and scientists. Nevertheless, Bush used his considerable administrative skills to speed scientific findings into the practical hands of manufacturers and then to the military for their use.

Two major developments credited to OSRD guidance were in radar and the proximity fuse. Although Bush wanted

Charles F. Kettering—"Dean of Inventors"

Charles F. Kettering (1876–1958), often referred to as the "Dean of Inventors," graduated from Ohio State University in 1904. He first worked for the National Cash Register Company, where he developed the electric cash register.

Forming Dayton Engineering Laboratories Company (Delco) in 1909, he developed the electric automobile starter that was first used by Cadillac in 1912. While running Delco he also invented the "Delco," a fuel-driven generator that electrified farms decades before power lines reached rural America. In 1916 Kettering sold his thriving business to General Motors (GM) and joined the staff. Overseeing its research facilities, Kettering remained at GM for thirty-one years. In 1927 he founded the Charles F. Kettering Foundation for research to benefit mankind.

During World War II (1939–45), "Boss Ket" headed the National Inventors Council that examined new inventions sent to the government. He also had a regular Sunday afternoon radio program that was listened to by millions of Americans. "Horsepower is war power" is the slogan he used on the program, as related in the December 1944 issue of *The National Geographic Magazine* in the article "Michigan Fights." A few other Kettering inventions included spark plugs, Freon for electric refrigerators, quick-drying automobile paint, automatic transmission, the first lightweight diesel locomotive engine, and the first synthetic aviation fuel. At the close of the war in 1945, Kettering, along with Alfred Sloan (1875–1966), founded the Sloan-Kettering Institute for Cancer Research. Located in New York City, it remained at the beginning of the twenty-first century a premier cancer research and treatment center.

At his death in 1958, Kettering held roughly 140 patents and had been presented honorary doctorate degrees by about thirty universities.

to use existing facilities, a few new facilities were established. The Radiation Laboratory was created at MIT and developed superior radar systems manufactured by Sperry, Westinghouse, Philco, and Bell Labs.

The proximity fuse is often credited with turning, then winning, the war for the Allies. The proximity fuse was a detonation device for setting off rockets, bombs, and later, torpedoes. The small fuse was guided by radar and was highly accurate in finding its target. It was first used in battle in January 1943. Manufactured by Sylvania, the fuse was developed

President Harry Truman presents the medal for Merit and Bronze Oak Leaf cluster to Dr. James Bryant Conant (right) and Dr. Vannevar Bush (left) on May 27, 1948. Bush and Conant received the medal for their achievements in atomic research during World War II. © *Bettmann/ Corbis. Reproduced by permission.*

through the Applied Physics Laboratory, Section T, at Johns Hopkins University with U.S. Navy procurement contracts. The fuse developed was a classic example of university, industry, and military cooperation. Other devices developed and manufactured through OSRD facilitation were underwater sonar used in antisubmarine warfare, amphibious landing vehicles, mine detectors, flame throwers, the bazooka rocket, other rockets, torpedoes, and chemical warfare products. Medical advances included the drug atabrine for treating malaria, DDT to kill disease-carrying insects, plasma transfusions, and psychiatric programs to deal with those traumatized by war.

Bush and the MIT Radiation Lab also became heavily involved in the Manhattan Project, the U.S. project to develop an atomic bomb. Ultimately Bush handed OSRD's involvement in nuclear development to the Army Corps of Engineers, but he and other OSRD scientists still oversaw much of the research.

Beginning of the National Science Foundation

As the war wound down, Bush had no political interest in establishing postwar government or military policies. However, he adamantly urged President Roosevelt by late 1944 and early 1945 to establish federal support for practical research in health and national security. Bush wanted to disband OSRD, since it had been widely funded by emergency war monies, and establish a permanent research foundation that he called the National Research Foundation.

After considerable wrangling over control and funding, Congress, in 1950, finally passed legislation that President Harry S. Truman (1884–1972; served 1945–53) signed. The name of the new foundation would be the National Science Foundation (NSF). It had a tiny budget as health funds went to the expanding National Institutes of Health and national security funds went to the military. Only after the Soviet Union launched Sputnik, the world's first satellite, in 1957 did the NSF become a major scientific research player. It then grew into one of the chief supporters of U.S. scientific endeavors throughout the rest of the twentieth century and into the twenty-first century.

Never slowed down

Meanwhile, in 1945 Bush published his article "As We May Think" in the magazine the *Atlantic Monthly.* Based on his visionary research on computerlike devices in the 1920s and 1930s, he described a theoretical device called a "memex" that would enhance human thought and hence research. In this article, Bush is credited with putting forth the first early thoughts on automation of the human thought processes or computerization.

Bush also headed the Research and Development Board from 1946 to 1949. He labored to untangle competing military rivalries and develop an economic and rational way for the nation to carry out national defense research. Bush resigned his post and returned to CIW in 1949. He also supported J. Robert Oppenheimer, the scientist known as the father of the atomic bomb, when he came under congressional investigation for alleged leaks to the Soviet Union. Both Bush and Oppenheimer vigorously opposed the development and testing of a hydrogen bomb.

In 1955 Bush retired from CIW. He served as trustee and on the boards of directors of various large corporations. He also continued his research in storing information, both for libraries and as learning enhancers. The use of microfilm continued as one of his chief interests. Bush died in Belmont, Massachusetts, in 1974. He had revolutionized the way universities, private industry, and government worked together in scientific research and development. The military-industrial-university complex that developed after World War II was largely based on examples set by the operations of Bush's OSRD.

For More Information

Books

Baxter, James P. *Scientists Against Time*. Cambridge, MA: MIT Press, 1968.

Buderi, Robert. *The Invention that Changed the World: How a Small Group of Radar Pioneers Won the Second World War and Launched a Technological Revolution*. New York: Simon and Schuster, 1996.

Burke, Colin B. *Information and Secrecy: Vannevar Bush, Ultra, and the Other Memex*. Metuchen, NJ: Scarecrow Press, 1994.

Conant, Jennet. *Tuxedo Park: A Wall Street Tycoon and the Secret Palace of Science that Changed the Course of World War II*. New York: Simon and Schuster, 2002.

Zachary, G. Pascal. *Endless Frontier: Vannevar Bush, Engineer of the American Century*. New York: Free Press, 1997.

Periodicals

"Yankee Scientist." *Time* (April 3, 1944), pp. 52–57.

Klemmer, Harvey. "Michigan Fights." *The National Geographic Magazine* (December 1944), pp. 676–715.

Web sites

Hall of Fame, Inventor Profile: Charles Franklin Kettering. http://www.invent.org/hall_of_fame/86.html (accessed on July 18, 2004).

Internet Pioneers: Vannevar Bush. http://www.ibiblio.org/pioneers/bush.html (accessed on July 18, 2004).

Kettering Foundation. http://www.kettering.org/History/history.html (accessed on July 18, 2004).

Office of Scientific Research and Development. http://history.acusd.edu/gen/WW2Timeline/OSRD.html (accessed on July 18, 2004).

James F. Byrnes

Born May 2, 1879
Charleston, South Carolina
Died April 9, 1972
Columbia, South Carolina

Secretary of state, U.S. senator, Supreme Court justice, governor

O ne of the few Americans to serve in all three branches of the federal government—as U.S. congressman and senator, Supreme Court justice, and secretary of state—James F. Byrnes became known as "assistant president on the home front" during World War II (1939–45). To guide wartime home front economic activities, President **Franklin D. Roosevelt** (1882–1945; served 1933–45; see entry) assigned Byrnes more powers than ever held by a public official. He was clearly one of the most powerful men in Washington through much of the 1940s.

"Roosevelt had declared 'Your decision is my decision, and . . . there is no appeal. For all practical purposes you will be assistant President.'"

—*From* Sly and Able: A Political Biography of James F. Byrnes

Humble beginnings

James Francis Byrnes was born in Charleston, South Carolina, to Irish immigrants. His official birth date is listed as May 2, 1879, though he was actually born on May 2, 1882. He changed his birth date so he could apply for work early in life. His father, a city clerk, died weeks before he was born, of tuberculosis at age twenty-six. His mother, Elizabeth McSweeney Byrnes, worked hard as a dressmaker to provide for Jimmy,

James F. Byrnes.
The Library of Congress.

as he was known throughout his life. The family made do and young Jimmy attended private Catholic school. However, Jimmy left school at age fourteen and found work as a messenger and later law clerk for a law office for the next seven years to help support the family. The circuit court in Aiken, South Carolina, hired Jimmy Byrnes at the age of twenty-one as a court stenographer (reporter). Judge James Aldrich and others in the court took personal interest in Byrnes and guided him through law studies. In only three years, in 1903, Byrnes successfully passed the South Carolina bar exam and began a private law practice in Aiken while remaining a court reporter.

In 1906 Byrnes married Maude Perkins Busch of Aiken. They would have no children. Byrnes quickly jumped into politics. He won his first public office in 1908 as a public prosecutor. Just two years later, in 1910, he won a seat in the U.S. House of Representatives as a Democratic candidate in a very close race.

Congressman Byrnes

Byrnes served as a U.S. congressman for the next fourteen years. He struck a very distinctive presence in the Washington power circles. He was short, thin, very energetic, and had sharp eyes. Though living modestly, he dressed well. Byrnes quickly gained the respect of other congressmen for his shrewd dealings in seeking compromises on issues to get legislation passed.

Byrnes had interests in several domestic issues. He was also a strong supporter of the newly created federal highway system. After his reelection in 1912, he became a member of the important House Appropriations Committee that oversees government funding. While working on naval funding issues, Byrnes formed a close friendship with a young Franklin D. Roosevelt, who was assistant secretary of the navy at the time, stationed in Washington, D.C. Typical of a white American from South Carolina in the 1910s, Byrnes believed in racial segregation (separation of races in public places) and worked to defeat anti-lynching bills introduced in Congress. (Lynching is the unlawful murder of black Americans by mob action.) Byrnes also fought women's right to vote, which was finally granted by constitutional amendment in 1920.

Having gained substantial prestige in the House, Byrnes ran for the U.S. Senate in 1924 but lost to a longstanding popular political figure in South Carolina. Byrnes suddenly found himself out of public office. He returned to a private law practice for the next six years in Spartanburg, South Carolina. During this time he kept his name before the South Carolina public through active participation in various civic affairs.

A rising political force

In 1930 the economic downturn of the Great Depression (1929–41) struck South Carolina hard. Unemployment rose as business activity slowed down. The door was opened for new political leaders. Seizing on this opportunity, Byrnes ran for the U.S. Senate again and won by a slim vote margin thanks to the support of wealthy financier and fellow South Carolinian Bernard Baruch. As he had earlier in the House, Byrnes quickly rose in the Senate to positions of power, becoming a member of various important committees.

Roosevelt was nominated the Democratic candidate for president in 1932, and Byrnes campaigned hard for his friend. After winning the election, Roosevelt used Byrnes as a key Democratic Senate leader to push New Deal legislation through Congress. The New Deal was President Roosevelt's program of economic relief and reform to help those most affected by the Great Depression. They successfully steered numerous programs through into reality. With their public popularity running high, both Roosevelt and Byrnes easily won reelection in 1936.

Byrnes had great ambitions for higher office given his successes in Congress and numerous friends in powerful positions. When Roosevelt decided to run for an unprecedented third term in 1940, Byrnes expected to be the president's running mate. Roosevelt selected Henry A. Wallace instead. However, Roosevelt soon turned to Byrnes for another important role. The president sought to have a Supreme Court more sympathetic to his New Deal programs when deciding legal challenges. When a position on the bench opened, Roosevelt appointed Byrnes to the U.S. Supreme Court in June 1941.

Donald Nelson

Within a month after the December 7, 1941, Japanese surprise attack on Pearl Harbor, Hawaii, and nine months before the Office of Economic Stabilization was created with Jimmy Byrnes its head, President Franklin D. Roosevelt (1882–1945; served 1933–45) created the War Production Board (WPB) to guide the war industry mobilization on the home front. The president turned to Donald Nelson (1888–1959) to lead this very important task.

Born in Hannibal, Missouri, Nelson graduated from the University of Missouri with a degree in chemical engineering. Hired as a chemist by Sears, Roebuck and Company in 1912, Nelson rose through the company ranks to become executive vice president in 1939. As the German military swept through Western Europe in early 1940, Roosevelt became increasingly eager to assist Great Britain and France in their effort to stop Germany. He appointed Nelson in May 1940 to a Treasury Department post in charge of handling requests from foreign nations for raw materials and war materials. After France fell to German forces in June 1940 and Britain came under relentless intense aerial bombing, concern increased about preparing the nation for possible war. In January 1941 Roosevelt created the Office of Production Management (OPM) with Nelson responsible for purchasing billions of dollars of materials for the defense industries. In July, to spur the flow of needed materials to military and war industries, Roosevelt created the Supply, Priorities, and Allocations Board (SPAB) with Nelson its director.

The Japanese bombing of Pearl Harbor and declaration of war led Roosevelt to create the WPB in January 1942. U.S. war production was placed under the guidance of one person, Nelson. Immediately Nelson began taking such dramatic actions as converting the automobile industry to the production of war planes, tanks, and military vehicles. Nelson also oversaw the allocation of such critical materials as steel and production of synthetic rubber. Nelson remained head of WPB until he resigned in August 1944. Nelson became Roosevelt's special representative on a trip to the Soviet Union and China before returning to private industry, where he served as chairman of the board for several mining and chemical companies until his death in September 1959.

Assistant president

Following the surprise Japanese attack on Pearl Harbor, Hawaii, on December 7, 1941, Byrnes quickly became restless hearing cases on the Supreme Court. He wanted an active part in the war effort. His opportunity came in October 1942 when

Roosevelt selected him to serve as head of the newly created Office of Economic Stabilization (OES), with his office located in the White House. As head of OES, Byrnes was responsible for keeping prices of consumer goods in check, developing a new tax plan to finance the war, and overseeing a new complex rationing program. It was a controversial position that he handled well. Most notably, he adopted the Controlled Materials Plan (CMP) that strictly controlled the distribution of aluminum, copper, and steel—three materials critical to war industries. The success of the CMP played a major role in getting war production underway.

As the war industries continued to gear up to full speed, disputes arose between industries and the War Production Board (WPB) over access to manpower and raw materials. The WPB had been created in January 1942, with Donald Nelson its head, to oversee the war mobilization of industry on the home front. Numerous disputes arose over access to raw materials and to workers as shortages began appearing by early 1943. In May 1943 Roosevelt created the Office of War Mobilization (OWM) with Byrnes its head to guide the WPB and resolve disputes. Byrnes now had responsibility for both the home front economy and industrial mobilization.

Byrnes, through these roles, became the second most powerful person in government next to Roosevelt, even referred to as "assistant president." While Roosevelt concentrated on the war and foreign diplomacy, Byrnes set domestic policies and coordinated all the federal agencies and the production, purchase, and distribution of all war materials. He oversaw everything from rationing to the scheduling of sporting events. This included control of prices for consumer goods, rent prices, wages, services, food production, and profits of war industries. He even controlled the availability of shoes to the public. Among these duties he also oversaw the Manhattan Project, the top secret program to develop the atomic bomb. He met with project scientists to discuss government policies toward the use of the atomic bomb. Some one hundred thousand people were involved in the Manhattan Project.

Once again Byrnes wanted to be Roosevelt's running mate for the 1944 elections and eventually become the real president. However, the Democratic Party selected Harry S. Truman (1884–1972; served 1945–53) instead because of

Byrnes's segregationist views and because labor did not like the restrictions on wages he imposed during the war.

In late 1944, in anticipation of the war's end, OWM was revamped into the Office of War Mobilization and Reconversion (OWMR) to oversee the transition back from industrial production of war materials to consumer goods. Byrnes remained its head. Businesses and government were eager to dispose of the now unneeded large manufacturing plants used for war production. Businesses were also eager to end the longstanding government contracts they had received to produce war materials.

Cold War negotiator

By 1945, with the home front war efforts winding down, Byrnes began applying his strong negotiating skills to assist President Roosevelt in foreign affairs. Through 1945 and 1946, Byrnes was a central figure in the developing Cold War

(1945–91) political and military rivalry between the United States and the Soviet Union. In February 1945 the president invited Byrnes to accompany him to a meeting with Soviet premier Joseph Stalin (1879–1953) and British prime minister Winston Churchill (1874–1965) at Yalta in the Soviet Union. The three world leaders discussed what postwar Europe should be like, particularly what to do about Germany. While at Yalta, Byrnes lunched daily with Roosevelt and took detailed notes of Roosevelt's accounts of his meetings with Stalin. Only two months later, President Roosevelt died suddenly of a cerebral hemorrhage. Vice President Truman became president and immediately called for Byrnes and his notes. The new president wanted to be consistent with Roosevelt's thoughts and private commitments made at Yalta. Truman also asked Byrnes to organize Roosevelt's funeral and appointed him secretary of state.

Byrnes accompanied Truman to the next meeting with leaders of Great Britain and the Soviet Union at Potsdam, Germany, in June 1945. Throughout the remainder of 1945, Byrnes was the key U.S. official at various high-level international meetings including a December meeting in Moscow. He remained confident his seasoned negotiating skills would lead to a productive relationship with the Soviets.

In Moscow, Byrnes made a last all-out effort to establish friendly relations with the Soviets. He made several deals concerning international control of atomic energy and the kinds of postwar governments that would exist in Bulgaria, Hungary, and Japan. The deals proved very unpopular when he returned to the United States. Many in Congress and the public charged that Byrnes gave in to the Communists. His political influence on the national stage would not recover.

Byrnes toughened his position toward the Soviets through 1946. He was even named *Time* magazine's Man of the Year in 1946. However, he could not overcome a growing personality conflict with Truman. Byrnes finally resigned as secretary of state in January 1947.

Governor Byrnes

Returning to South Carolina, Byrnes won election as governor of South Carolina in 1950, receiving 85 percent of the vote. Disagreeing with Truman's and the Democratic

Party's opposition to racial segregation, like many Southerners in the early 1950s Byrnes switched political party membership to the Republican Party. Byrnes was particularly interested in improving public education in South Carolina for both white and black Americans as well as establishing programs for mentally handicapped black children. However, he remained resistant to public school integration, which directly led to the landmark 1954 U.S. Supreme Court decision in *Brown v. Board of Education.* The case combined a South Carolina case with several other cases. The decision banned racial segregation in public schools. Byrnes retired from office in 1955 and died on April 9, 1972, in Columbia, South Carolina. In January 1982 Byrnes became the twenty-fourth person inducted to the South Carolina Hall of Fame.

For More Information

Books

Brown, Walter J. *James F. Byrnes of South Carolina: A Remembrance.* Macon, GA: Mercer University Press, 1991.

Byrnes, James F. *All in One Lifetime.* New York: Harper, 1958.

Curry, George F. *James F. Byrnes.* New York: Cooper Square, 1965.

Robertson, David. *Sly and Able: A Political Biography of James F. Byrnes.* New York: Norton, 1994.

Periodicals

"Nelson, the Coordinator." *Business Week* (January 31, 1942): p. 18.

Web sites

The Byrnes Scholarships. http://www.byrnesscholars.org (accessed on July 18, 2004).

Frank Capra

Born May 18, 1897
Bisacquino, Sicily
Died September 3, 1991
La Quinta, California

Film director

Frank Capra was one of the most famous American film directors in the twentieth century. Three times he earned Academy Awards for best director for the movies *It Happened One Night* (1934), *Mr. Deeds Goes to Town* (1936), and *You Can't Take It With You* (1938). During World War II (1939–45), Capra produced the film series *Why We Fight* for the U.S. War Department. His military service earned him the Distinguished Service Medal, the highest American military decoration for non-combat service.

As a film director, Capra was a poet of the personal and the moral rather than the social and the political. He focused on the way individuals react to situations and each other rather than on the situation itself. People responded to his films because they were idealistic, patriotic, and full of optimism. The 1930s had been a dark decade due to the economic hardships of the Great Depression (1929–41), and people were looking to escape the despair surrounding them. Capra's war films celebrated common people and their all-American values. His films were simplistic and suited the spirit of the times.

"As with many other workers in the Hollywood feature film industry, Capra devoted his talents and energies toward serving his country during World War II."

—Charles J. Maland in his book Frank Capra

Frank Capra.
© *Bettmann/Corbis.*
Reproduced by permission.

Coming to America

Francesco Capra was born on May 18, 1897, in Bisacquino, Sicily, at the family home facing the church of his patron saint, San Francesco di Paola. His father, Salvatore Capra, was called Turiddu, the Italian equivalent of Sammy. His mother, Rosaria Nicolosi, was called Sara or Saridda Capra. When Frank was six years old, his peasant parents took him and his three siblings to America on a French steerage ship called the SS *Germania.* In thirteen days the family landed at Ellis Island in New York before making the cross-country trip that reunited them with Frank's older brother in Los Angeles, California. In 1903 the city was a vast stretch of fruit orchards and vegetable fields populated by less than two hundred thousand people. The neighborhoods where the Capras settled comprised a mix of ethnic groups, including Russian Jews, Armenians, Greeks, Germans, Irish, Orientals, Mexicans, Italians, and black Americans.

Frank worked his way through grammar school and high school and then the California Institute of Technology in Pasadena, where he graduated with a degree in chemical engineering in June 1918. The world was at war when he graduated from college and Frank enlisted at the U.S. Army recruiting station with the hopes of serving abroad. However, he was assigned to teach ballistic mathematics to artillery officers at Fort Mason in San Francisco. When World War I (1914–18) ended, jobs were scarce and Frank could not find an engineering job. He worked around the West Coast selling books, tutoring students, and doing odd jobs for a living. He became a naturalized American citizen in 1920 and registered his legal name as Frank Russell Capra.

Hollywood

In 1922 Frank Capra talked his way into directing a one-reel, short film titled *Fultah Fisher's Boarding House.* This was the beginning of his rise through the ranks in Hollywood. In 1927 he went to work as a company director for Columbia Pictures, located off Sunset Boulevard on Poverty Row, where funding was severely limited. Silent films were disappearing in favor of "talkies" (movies with sound) and Capra was to make Columbia's first sound picture in 1928. He became known as a reliable craftsman of efficient and profitable productions. His comedies always contained aspects of the improbable, the fantastic, and the unexpected. Part of Capra's mastery of the film medium was his success in allowing the viewer to experience what the actors were experiencing. It left the audience with the feeling that life was both miraculous and wonderful. His genre (type of film) of choice was comedy because he always wanted happy endings.

Capra married Lucille Warner Reyburn in 1932 and the two began a family. In 1930 Capra left Columbia Pictures and formed his own production company with Robert Riskin, the principal writer with whom Capra would produce most of his major films. They called their company Frank Capra Productions. Their first film, *Meet John Doe* (1941), was a relative box office disappointment. The filming of the company's last film *Arsenic And Old Lace,* began in 1941 but, due to the outbreak of war, would not be released until 1944.

Why We Fight

On December 12, 1941, five days after the devastating Japanese surprise attack on U.S. military bases at Pearl Harbor, Hawaii, Frank Capra was back in the army. He joined the Signal Corps with a major's commission. As a leading motion picture director of the time, he was called on to devote his filmmaking talent to the American effort, aimed at improving army morale. His unit of Special Services was only one of many government film units in existence at the time. His project, the *Why We Fight* films, would ultimately cost about four hundred thousand dollars, or less than 1 percent of the fifty million dollars the War Department spent on films during the war. Most of the army's filmmaking budget was being spent on combat photography and training films.

The Army Orientation Course was organized in 1940 in order to give the typical American GI an overview of the war. Presented in a series of pamphlets and fifteen lectures, it was a factual but rather dull approach to education that left most recruits uninspired. General George C. Marshall (1880–1959) realized that film was the best medium for providing information and affecting people. In 1942 he called on Capra, a great storyteller, to show the new draftees what they

America Speaks Films

In addition to informational movies produced by the military for wartime needs during World War II (1939–45), such as the *Why We Fight* series by Frank Capra, the Office of War Information (OWI), under the guidance of playwright Sam Spewack (1899–1971) also made government informational films. The OWI films played up U.S. successes on the home front, such as the miracles of industrial production. Many of these movies proved very popular with the public. Included were fifty-two informational short films called the *America Speaks* series. These OWI films were also known as *Victory Films.* Half of the series was written by the OWI staff; Hollywood studios wrote the other half.

The *America Speaks* films were to be shown at movie theaters along with the regular movie features. The OWI, through its Bureau of Motion Pictures, also made 16-mm films for showing at community centers such as schools and churches. These films proved very popular and reached a large audience. By the beginning of 1943, almost five million people had seen OWI film productions at more than thirty-one thousand showings.

were fighting for. Capra went to the New York Museum of Modern Art and watched all of the German Nazi propaganda (information designed to shape public opinions, usually by a government) films in their collection. The most important film he viewed was Leni Riefenstahl's *Triumph des Willens (Triumph of the Will)*. The film showed the Nazi's 1934 Nuremberg Party Congress with mythic imagery. Capra considered it the greatest propaganda film anyone had ever made. Riefenstahl used staged events along with music and her editing skills to create a powerful film that was such a psychological weapon it would motivate a nation and terrify an enemy. Capra decided to copy her style.

His experience from the early days working for Columbia Pictures on Poverty Row would come in handy during Capra's wartime service. Due to budget constraints most of Capra's films were made out of existing footage. Some came from newsreels and other propaganda and combat films, and some came from Hollywood entertainment films. There were also re-creations of newspaper headlines and animated

war maps. Capra was responsible for producing a series of motion pictures that explained the war to the common soldier while motivating each one to fight. He showed them what the enemy was capable of as well as what they stood to lose personally and as a nation, should the battle be lost. Capra used his expert editing skills in the films he was creating to simultaneously show differences between the forces of good and the forces of evil. The films provided a means of highlighting the moral battle Americans faced. Along the way, Capra received several promotions for his efforts.

Capra's *Why We Fight* series for the War Department began with the Oscar-winning film *Prelude to War*. The series originally was not intended for screening to the general public, but after General Marshall saw the rough-cut of *Prelude to War* in August 1942, he told Capra the film should be shown to the public. President **Franklin D. Roosevelt** (1882–1945; served 1933–45; see entry) agreed. Even British prime minister Winston Churchill (1874–1965) ordered that all of the films be

Lt. Colonel Frank Capra (right) poses with fellow military men (left to right): Captain A. Veiller, Captain John Huston, and Major Hugh Stewart. Capra received an Oscar for the first in a series of films entitled *Why We Fight,* which he produced for the War Department. *© Bettmann/ Corbis. Reproduced by permission.*

shown in British theaters and recorded a foreword for British audiences under Capra's direction.

The films *The Nazis Strike, Divide and Conquer*, and *The Battle of Britain* were produced in 1943. *The Battle of Russia* and *The Battle of China* followed in 1944. The series was completed when *War Comes to America* came out in 1945. After screening his films at the Pentagon, Capra would take them to the White House in the evening to view them with the president and Secretary of War **Henry L. Stimson** (1867–1950; see entry).

Capra's film unit completed a wide variety of projects before his discharge in June 1945. However, the *Why We Fight* series revolutionized documentary filmmaking and military training methods. On the day before he left Washington, Marshall summoned Capra into his office and pinned the Distinguished Service Medal on him. The citation stated, "The films produced by Colonel Capra under the direction of the Chief of Staff had an important influence on the morale of the Army. Colonel Capra also rendered an important service as Chief of the Army Motion Picture Unit and as Assistant Chief of the Army Pictorial Service."

Going home

After four years in the military, Frank Capra returned to Hollywood and an uncertain future. He and a group of other prominent directors cofounded the independent production company Liberty Pictures. For its first film the company reunited director Capra with actor Jimmy Stewart (1908–1997), who was also returning to Hollywood from service as a decorated pilot in the Air Corps. Liberty Pictures produced the film *It's A Wonderful Life*, which continued to be shown each Christmas in the United States into the twenty-first century. It was Capra's favorite film, but it was not a commercial success when released in 1946. In 1948 Liberty Pictures was sold to Paramount.

By the late 1940s and early 1950s, Capra found theaters no longer full and his optimistic spirit no longer in tune with the spirit of the times. Capra had a record of deeply felt patriotism toward his adopted country. To his personal dismay, he was investigated as a Communist by the House Un-American Activities Committee (HUAC) and was called to testify against others in the movie industry. The government feared that Communism had infiltrated America during the war and was especially concerned about Hollywood because of its influence on the nation. The elements of social criticism in Capra's films, along with his personal and professional associations in the business, cast suspicion on him during this postwar period.

Capra retired to La Quinta, California, where he wrote his autobiography and toured colleges lecturing on films. In 1982 he was awarded the American Film Institute's Life Achievement Award. His beloved wife, Lucille, died in 1984. Capra suffered a stroke in 1985 and remained in poor health until his death in La Quinta on September 3, 1991.

For More Information

Books

Capra, Frank. *The Name above the Title*. New York: Da Capo Press, 1971.

Maland, Charles J. *Frank Capra*. Boston: Twayne, 1980.

McBride, Joseph. *Frank Capra: The Catastrophe of Success*. New York: Simon & Schuster, 1992.

Poague, Leland A. *The Cinema of Frank Capra*. Cranbury, NJ: A. S. Barnes and Co., 1975.

Schickel, Richard. *The Men Who Made the Movies*. New York: Educational Broadcasting Corporation, 1975.

Web sites

"Frank Capra." *University of San Diego, History Department*. http://history.acusd.edu/gen/filmnotes/capra.html (accessed on July 21, 2004).

Elmer Davis

Born January 13, 1890
Aurora, Indiana
Died May 18, 1958
Washington, D.C.

Federal administrator, radio commentator, news reporter

"Our job at home is to give the American people the fullest possible understanding of what this war is about . . . not only to tell the American people how the war is going, but where it is going and where it came from."

Elmer Davis.
AP/Wide World Photos.
Reproduced by permission.

Elmer Davis, a popular national radio newscaster, became director of the newly formed Office of War Information (OWI), charged with coordinating government information about World War II's (1939–45) progress to the home front. It was a role that placed him in continual confrontation with U.S. military leaders concerning what the public had a right to know.

A desire to learn

Elmer Davis was born on January 13, 1890, in the southeast Indiana town of Aurora. He was raised in a family that valued education and knowledge. His father, Elam H. Davis, was a cashier at the First National Bank of Aurora, and his mother, Louise Severin, was a high school principal. During his early school years, Elmer became known for an inquiring mind, always searching for information, and for being a good writer and avid reader. He began his career in newspapers during the summer after his freshman year of high school, when he got a job as a printer's devil for the Aurora *Bulletin*. Printer's devils had the very messy job of setting type and handling ink-covered materials. Elmer also began writing stories, selling his first one for twenty-five dollars to the Indianapolis *Star.* He attended Franklin College, located twenty miles south of Indianapolis, beginning at age sixteen. He served as the school correspondent for the *Star.*

Upon graduation from Franklin in 1910, Elmer Davis received a Rhodes scholarship to Oxford University in England. He quickly began distinguishing himself in his studies at the prestigious English educational institution. Davis completed his studies in two years and toured Europe, learning of its geography, politics, and history, which would be useful to him later in his news career. However, in 1913 he received word from home that his father was very ill. He returned to Aurora, but too late, as his father died while he was on his way.

A writing career

With few job opportunities in Aurora, Davis landed a job as editor for *Adventure* magazine in New York City, making ten dollars a week. After a year he was hired as a reporter for the *New York Times,* where he covered a wide variety of stories for the next ten years such as championship boxing matches, political conventions, and religious rallies. In 1917 he married Florence MacMillan of Mount Vernon, New York, whom he met earlier while on his journeys through Europe. They would have two children.

Davis rose in position to editorial writer for the *Times* while the United States fought in World War I (1914–18). In December 1923 Davis left the *Times* to pursue a freelance writing career. Settling into a summer home in Mystic, Connecticut, he was very successful writing both fiction and nonfiction for a number of popular magazines. These included the *Saturday Review of Literature, Harper's, New Republic, Liberty Magazine,* and *Collier's.* He also wrote fictional books and filled in at times as a newscaster on CBS radio.

Radio personality

In 1939 while writing a serial mystery novel for *The Saturday Evening Post,* the news department director of Columbia Broadcasting System (CBS) called and offered Davis a job as radio news analyst. He took the place of popular newscaster H. V. Kaltenborn, who went on assignment to Europe to cover the unfolding events of Germany's military expansion. Davis often worked eighteen hours a day covering European events from the CBS studios, though he was only on the air for one hour a day.

Davis became very popular with CBS listeners. His Midwest accent and direct approach without many frills, in contrast to other radio newscasters of the time, gave a "back home" feel to his broadcasts. Millions of listeners tuned in regularly to his daily reports.

Office of War Information

On March 2, 1942, Davis gave a strongly stated broadcast urging the U.S. government to greatly improve its ability to get war news to the public. Frustrated, he claimed too many agencies were involved in controlling information. There was the Office of Facts and Figures, the Office of Government Reports, the Office of Emergency Management's Division of Information, and the Office of Co-Ordinator of Information. He called for a single agency headed by a single person to coordinate information to the public. The *New Yorker* magazine quickly came to support Davis's observations and wrote that Davis should be that person.

In reaction to the growing public dissatisfaction with the government's control of war information, on June 13, 1942, President **Franklin D. Roosevelt** (1882–1945; served 1933–45; see entry) created the Office of War Information (OWI). It combined the responsibilities of all existing federal information offices. He appointed Davis as its director. Davis left his CBS post and saw his income drop from fifty-three thousand dollars to twelve thousand dollars. As head of the OWI, Davis oversaw the production of radio messages, leaflets, booklets, films, and a glossy magazine titled *Victory*. In addition, Davis sought to make sure the entertainment industry was providing to the public a positive image through their productions. Movies and radio programs were to be inspiring and showing confidence in a future beyond war. Davis, through the OWI, sought to highlight the positive aspects of the American way of life.

The OWI had an annual budget of twenty-five million dollars and employed thirty thousand people with diverse skills, including news editors, advertising experts, poets, film directors, lawyers, anthropologists, sociologists, playwrights, and film directors. In Washington, the OWI had offices in the Library of Congress, Social Security Building, and U.S. Information Building. Though not having developed administrative skills in the past, Davis molded a very effective organization. He was always answering to independent-minded writers and others who did not want to become simply propagandists for the government. Davis contended relentlessly that the public should know as much as possible about the progress of the war, balanced with the need for certain amounts of military secrecy.

Davis worked with film, radio, music, and printed material. He established the Domestic Radio Bureau to provide war information over the airwaves. One radio program series,

CBS news analyst Elmer Davis watches the news tickers for the latest developments on the battlefronts during World War II. *© Bettmann/Corbis. Reproduced by permission.*

Bureau of Motion Pictures

A key responsibility of Elmer Davis and the Office of War Information (OWI) in 1942 was to coordinate the production of government information films and oversee Hollywood movie production. To accomplish this broad task, Davis created the Bureau of Motion Pictures (BMP) branch of the OWI. White House assistant Lowell Mellett was selected to head the BMP, which had offices in Washington, D.C., New York, and Los Angeles.

Playwright Sam Spewack (1899–1971), head of the New York office, was responsible for making government informational films. The films focused on the good news related to the early war effort, such as the miraculous home front industrial production that was in high gear by late 1942. One such film, *Autobiography of a Jeep,* chronicled the life of an army jeep, a uniquely American war product, from production to use. Highly popular with the public, this film was released in sixteen different languages. BMP produced a series of fifty-two informational short films called *America Speaks.* Davis's OWI staff wrote half of the films, also known as *Victory Films,* and Hollywood screenwriters wrote the others. The films were shown in movie theaters around the country. However, even more people watched BMP 16-mm films about the war effort on the battlefield and the home front. The BMP provided the movies for showings at churches, schools, and other community buildings. By January 1943, the

Uncle Sam Speaks, included a character named Uncle Sam (representing the United States) speaking to listeners about hope for the future after the war. Other series included voice documentaries in which common citizens described their perspectives on different war issues and a series titled *The Man Behind the Gun* about American servicemen. The OWI also coordinated production of short spot announcements for war bonds, scrap drives, and V-mail that appeared in everything from kids' afternoon radio serial programs to the evening adventure dramas.

The OWI also worked with the Songwriters War Committee to produce informational songs promoting home front participation in scrap drives, victory gardens, and air

BMP films had more than thirty-one thousand showings to some 4.7 million people.

The Los Angeles BMP office, under the leadership of Nelson Poynter, reviewed Hollywood scripts and films before their release to make sure they presented the proper images to American citizens about the virtues of the American way of life. Some 1,650 movie scripts were voluntarily submitted for review. The BMP would often suggest inserting an inspirational war message at some point in the movie dialogue. In a few cases it recommended withholding the movie until after the war.

The BMP also coordinated informational films produced by the military. Perhaps the most popular military films on the home front were a series of films titled *Why We Fight* made by noted Hollywood director **Frank Capra** (1897–1991; see entry) for the U.S. Army. Originally created to be shown to newly recruited soldiers, they became so popular among the U.S. military leaders that the BMP made them available to the general public, too. The first film in the series, titled *Prelude to War* (1942), explained the events in Europe and Asia leading to war, the military dictatorships of Germany and Japan, and the reasons for going to war. Capra effectively included captured enemy newsreels in the film. The BMP made these inspirational films available to war industry workers and at community centers and movie theaters. BMP film production ceased in mid-1943 when Congress cut its funding.

raid drills. They also sought to boost the morale of war industry workers who were working long hours.

Davis's job was very demanding and controversial. Regarding the release of war news, Davis had to deal relentlessly with uncooperative military leaders. He also faced accusations by conservatives that his agency housed Communist sympathizers. In addition, congressional Republicans charged that the articles in *Victory* magazine, like many of OWI's films, focused too much on Roosevelt. They claimed the OWI materials served to rally public support for Roosevelt's potential 1944 reelection bid. In May 1943 Congress significantly reduced OWI funding. This stopped most of its home front programs. The OWI ceased operation in September 1945 after the surrender of Japan ended the war.

A defender of constitutional freedoms

After the war Davis returned to radio broadcasting, working for the American Broadcasting Company (ABC). When U.S. senator Joseph McCarthy (1908–1957) rose to prominence in 1950 by charging Communist influences in U.S. government and other segments of society, Davis led opposition to McCarthy's intimidation tactics. By the fall of 1953, Davis became so concerned about McCarthy's influence on America that he went on a speaking tour across the nation plugging the constitutional freedoms of speech and association. Much as he had done with OWI, he urged calm and reason among the public. Davis drew both extreme praise and criticism for his outspokenness. The speeches were compiled into a popular book titled *But We Were Born Free,* published the following year in 1954. The book sold one hundred thousand copies. The Senate finally voted to censor McCarthy in December 1954.

Davis was also greatly concerned about the proliferation (spreading) of nuclear weapons by the United States and the Soviet Union as the Cold War escalated in the 1950s. The Cold War was an intense political and economic rivalry from 1945 to 1991 between the United States and the Soviet Union, falling just short of military conflict. Davis wrote a number of articles about the perils of the nuclear arms race. They were published in various popular magazines. He combined the articles into a second book titled *Two Minutes Till Midnight* in 1955.

The various political battles took their toll on Davis. By the mid-1950s his health declined steadily and he gradually faded from the public eye. A year after his second book was released, Davis had to leave broadcasting. He suffered a stroke in March 1958 and was hospitalized at George Washington University Hospital in Washington, D.C., until he died on May 18 of that year.

For More Information

Books

Burlingame, Roger. *Don't Let Them Scare You: The Life and Times of Elmer Davis.* Philadelphia, PA: Lippincott, 1961.

Davis, Elmer H. *But We Were Born Free*. Indianapolis, IN: Bobbs-Merrill, 1954.

Davis, Elmer H. *Two Minutes Till Midnight*. Indianapolis, IN: Bobbs-Merrill, 1955.

Winkler, Allan M. *The Politics of Propaganda: The Office of War Information, 1942–1945*. New Haven, CT: Yale University Press, 1978.

Web sites

"Elmer Davis: Defender of American Liberties." *Indiana Historical Society.* http://www.indianahistory.org/pub/traces/edavis.html (accessed on July 21, 2004).

Donald Douglas

Born April 6, 1892
Brooklyn, New York
Died February 1, 1981
Santa Monica, California

Aircraft engineer, industrial executive

"The development of the airplane in the days between the wars is the greatest engineering story there ever was, and in the heart of it was Donald Douglas."

—Fortune *magazine, March 1941*

Donald Douglas.
© *Bettmann/Corbis.*
Reproduced by permission.

Donald Douglas is one of the most famous aircraft builders in the history of aviation. Although he never personally obtained a pilot's license, Douglas became fascinated with the idea of flight after he saw Orville Wright (1871–1948) fly a plane in 1909. He was a brilliant engineer and a shrewd businessman but he also had the rare gift of vision. Douglas was a pioneer in the technology that would introduce global air transportation and change world travel. While ocean liners required weeks to span the globe, airliners measured distances in hours.

In 1924 Douglas was responsible for the design and production of the first airplane capable of cross-continental flight, the Douglas World Cruiser. His company produced a continuing line of civil and military aircraft including the legendary DC-3. His commercial airliners set the industry standard for reliability and safety. His combat aircraft, consisting of relatively small attack bombers, helped win World War II (1939–45) by sinking many Japanese ships in the Pacific.

A born leader

Donald Willis Douglas was born on April 6, 1892, in Brooklyn, New York, the second son born to William and Dorothy Hagen-Locher Douglas. William was a cashier in a Wall Street bank and passed on his love of sailing to his sons. From his mother, Donald inherited his determination and enthusiasm for life.

Young Donald was intrigued by early attempts at flying, but when powered flight became a reality on December 17, 1903, he followed closely the advances made by the Wright brothers. He was present on July 30, 1909, when Orville Wright made his final tests to qualify the Wright Flyer for acceptance by the U.S. Army. His fascination with flight was confirmed. Upon graduation from Trinity Chapel preparatory school in the spring of 1909, Donald decided he could best advance his two great loves, airplanes and the sea, by attending the U.S. Naval Academy at Annapolis, Maryland. His older brother, Harold, graduated from the academy in 1911, but the following year Donald dropped out, convinced that aeronautical engineering was the right course for him.

Donald Douglas transferred to the Massachusetts Institute of Technology (MIT), the nation's top engineering school, and became its first aeronautical student. Having lost his three years of credit from the academy, he vowed to graduate from the four-year MIT program in two years. He succeeded, receiving his degree in 1914.

Moving on up

Douglas began his professional career in aviation working as chief engineer for the Glenn L. Martin Aircraft Company in Los Angeles, California. The company was building military planes near Griffith Park. While working at Martin, Douglas met a young registered nurse, Charlotte Marguerite Ogg. The couple soon married. They had four sons and one daughter.

In 1916 Douglas took a leave of absence to become the chief civilian aeronautical engineer for the U.S. Army Signal Corps. The experience became an education in federal

The ABCs of Military Planes

The military services labeled their aircraft types with a combination letter and numbering system, such as P-47, B-17, A-29, or C-130. The letters indicated the type of missions the plane was designed for. The following list provides some examples:

PT—Primary Trainer
BT—Basic Trainer
AT—Advanced Trainer
P—Pursuit (fighter)
B—Bomber
A—Assault
C—Cargo

paperwork and its accompanying delays. Aviation was still in its infancy in the United States, whereas in Europe rapid strides were being made. Despite Douglas's best efforts, the government failed to understand the future importance of air power and continued to show an official lack of interest. Frustrated, Douglas left Washington, D.C., after a year, knowing that America had entered World War I (1914–18) woefully short of planes and pilots.

In 1918 Douglas returned to work for Glenn Martin, this time in Cleveland, Ohio, where Martin had moved his operations. With the nation still at war, Douglas drew on his Washington contacts to help his company win a production contract for its newly developed twin-engine bomber, the Martin M-1. The airplane helped the Martin Aircraft Company survive after the end of the war, which saw 90 percent of the aircraft industry go out of business.

A company is born

Though it had been more than a decade since the Wright brothers' patent was approved, few yet dared to risk investing in what was still essentially a cottage industry (up-and-coming businesses with little investment). Years of research and testing, along with a great deal of money and determination, would be required to move the venture forward. Despite the challenges, Douglas still wanted to establish his own company. A motivating factor in his decision was a conviction that the airplane had a bright future as a mode of civilian transport. To most businesspeople in 1920 the aircraft industry did not look promising for investment, as few people flew and still fewer built airplanes.

With less than one thousand dollars in his pocket, Douglas moved his family to Southern California in 1920.

He soon joined forces with wealthy Los Angeles sportsman David R. Davis to establish the Davis-Douglas Aircraft Company. Davis wanted to gain fame by becoming the first person to fly nonstop across the United States. Douglas designed a plane that was dubbed the Cloudster. It was the first plane able to carry a payload exceeding its own weight. Although it failed in its intended mission, the Cloudster became the basis of the U.S. Navy's first torpedo bomber. Davis withdrew from the partnership and Douglas set up his own company, the Douglas Aircraft Company. Douglas soon earned a reputation as a master aircraft builder. He attracted the best talent in the country to work for him. The company grew steadily, building planes for the army air corps, the army, and the U.S. Post Office in the 1920s. In the 1930s he began work on the famous DC (Douglas Commercial) series of transport and passenger planes, including the DC-3, which revolutionized air travel. The 21-passenger DC-3 had great dependability and flew very economically with its sleek, low-wing design. President **Franklin D. Roosevelt** (1882–1945; served 1933–45; see entry) presented the prestigious Robert J. Collier Trophy to Donald Douglas in 1936 for the plane's design and called it the greatest achievement in U.S. aviation.

Drawn into war

When Japanese warplanes attacked Pearl Harbor, Hawaii, on December 7, 1941, the U.S. Navy was crippled. Americans expected an attack on the Pacific Coast to follow at any time. The shores were patrolled constantly in search of the enemy. General Douglas MacArthur (1880–1964), head of the U.S. armed forces in the Pacific area at the time, was stationed in the Philippines. Believing that the Japanese were focusing on the U.S. mainland, MacArthur took no defensive measures to ensure that planes and equipment at Clark Air Field in the Philippines were out of harm's way. Nine days after Pearl Harbor the Japanese staged a full-scale attack on the Philippines, wiping out American air power in the Pacific.

After the two attacks, the Army Air Force had only eleven hundred planes fit for combat. Many of those were slow and outdated. The best available fighter planes could not even reach the cruising altitude of enemy bombers. At the start of

Boeing Aircraft

On August 1, 1997, McDonnell–Douglas merged with Douglas's old rival, Boeing Aircraft, to form the world's largest aerospace company. It was one of the few aviation pioneers still in business in the twenty-first century and was one of only two major commercial aircraft manufacturers in the world in 2003. The newly combined company primarily competed with the Airbus Industrie, a European consortium, for major projects.

William Boeing, a Seattle, Washington, timber magnate and ship manufacturer, believed he could build a better plane than what he saw in 1914. At that time, he flew as a passenger in an early Curtiss Flying Boat off nearby Lake Washington. In 1916 he and a partner, Conrad Westervedt, produced the B&W floatplane. It performed well enough for them to incorporate their new business as the Pacific Aero Products Company. The company was contracted to manufacture airplanes during World War I (1914–18). It would continue as a military supplier throughout its history under its new name, the Boeing Airplane Company. However, little demand for planes existed after the war. The company turned its efforts to manufacturing boats and furniture. It used its existing aircraft to become the first to fulfill a U.S. Post Office Foreign Air Mail contract, delivering mail between Seattle,

1942 America was fighting two air wars, in Europe and in Asia, and it was not prepared for either.

As a result, World War II saw a huge increase in airplane production. Home front factories and shipyards worked twenty-four hours a day, seven days a week to deliver the necessary equipment to its military forces. One Douglas factory alone was producing a plane every hour. Over the course of the war, Douglas built nearly 30,000 planes with its wartime work force of 160,000 employees.

Five hundred DC-3s were delivered to Pearl Harbor. Throughout the course of the war, various military versions of the plane served in every conceivable transport role on every front. They bore roughly 70 percent of the total Allied air traffic throughout the war. When the last DC-3 was built in 1946,

Washington, and Victoria, British Columbia, Canada. In 1929 Boeing consolidated its operations into a holding company (a company that manages other companies) called United Aircraft and Transport Company. This situation lasted only until 1934, when the federal government took legal action to break up holding companies based on antitrust concerns (limiting competition in the marketplace). Boeing Air Transport went back to its roots manufacturing airplanes.

In 1931 Boeing developed the Boeing 247 that went into service in 1933. It is considered one of the first modern airliners because of its all-aluminum exterior, faster speed, low-mounted wing, and retractable landing gear. With the advent of transoceanic flights, Boeing introduced its 314 flying boat in 1939. Military application for the large aircraft was suddenly needed when the United States entered World War II (1939–45) in 1941. In response, the company developed large bombers, the B-17 and the B-29, to meet military needs.

The jet engine was developed during World War II but its cost was prohibitive until a commercial use could be established. In the 1950s Douglas and Boeing contended to build the first American jet passenger airliner. Boeing took the lead with its four-engine 707 in 1958. The smaller capacity model 727 and 737 would follow in the 1960s. The Boeing jets would be used around the world for decades.

the total production amounted to 803 civil airliners and 10,123 military versions to carry troops and cargo.

Changing times

After helping his company play a critical role in the war effort, Douglas shifted his focus to commercial aviation, missile production, and space vehicles in the following two decades. He remained president of the Douglas Aircraft Company until 1957, when Douglas passed day-to-day operations over to his son, though continuing in his role as chairman of the board. In the 1960s Douglas's competitor Boeing gained dominance in the commercial aviation market. Douglas had lost its big market share.

Bombers being assembled at the Douglas Aircraft Plant in Long Beach, California, in 1942. *Courtesy of the FDR Library.*

In 1967 Douglas merged his company with St. Louis, Missouri-based McDonnell Aircraft Corporation. Douglas served as honorary chairman of the board of the newly formed McDonnell–Douglas Company. After his retirement he remained active in the aerospace community, receiving many honors from across the world. Douglas Aircraft was also inducted into the International Aerospace Hall of Fame in 1967.

An enthusiastic sailor throughout his life, Douglas cherished a silver medal he won for sailing in the 1932 Olympic Games in Los Angeles. Douglas died on February 1, 1981, at the age of eighty-eight. In keeping with his lifelong love for the sea, his ashes were scattered over the Pacific Ocean.

For More Information

Books

Heppenheimer, T. A. *A Brief History of Flight: From Balloons to Mach 3 and Beyond*. New York: John Wiley & Sons, 2001.

Howard, Frank, and Bill Gunston. *The Conquest of the Air*. New York: Random House, 1972.

Morrison, Wilbur H. *Donald W. Douglas: A Heart with Wings*. Ames, IA: Iowa State University Press, 1991.

Van der Linden, F. Robert. *The Boeing 247: The First Modern Airliner*. Seattle, WA: University of Washington Press, 1991.

Verges, Marianne. *On Silver Wings*. New York: Random House, 1991.

Periodicals

"The North American Way." *Fortune* (March 1941): pp. 99–103.

Web sites

"Chasing the Sun—Donald Douglas." *Public Broadcasting System*. http://www.pbs.org/kcet/chasingthesun/innovators/ddouglas.html (accessed on July 21, 2004).

"Donald Douglas." *U.S. Centennial of Flight Commission*. http://www.1903to2003.gov/essay/Dictionary/douglas/DI130.htm (accessed on July 21, 2004).

Betty Grable

Born December 18, 1916
St. Louis, Missouri
Died July 2, 1973
Santa Monica, California

Model, actress

"Betty was a representation of the girl-back-home for thousands of homesick young lads. . . . She was company on a cold night, comfort at times of pain."

—*From* Betty Grable: The Reluctant Movie Queen

Betty Grable.
© *Bettmann/Corbis.*
Reproduced by permission.

A Hollywood movie studio dubbed the 1943 pinup of actress Betty Grable "the picture that launched a million dreams." The term "pinup" was coined to describe the photographs of female actresses and singers that would decorate the barracks and planes of countless soldiers during World War II (1939–45). Entertainers remaining on the home front during the war used their celebrity in a variety of ways to advance the war effort. The most famous pinup to come out of World War II was Grable's. Her photograph, showing Grable from behind in a bathing suit, peering over her shoulder and smiling playfully with her hands on her hips, represented the girl back on the home front for thousands of homesick soldiers and reminded them daily of what they were fighting for. It is regarded as second in popularity among wartime photographs only to the American flag-raising scene at Iwo Jima.

A star is born

Ruth Elizabeth Grable was born on December 18, 1916, in St. Louis, Missouri. She was the third child born to Lillian Hofman and John Conn Grable. One son, John, died early in 1916.

Betty's father, who went by the name Conn, was a stockbroker, and her mother focused her energy on show business aspirations for her daughters. When Betty's older sister Marjorie showed a lack of talent and interest, all of Lillian's attention shifted to Betty. Betty was enrolled in a variety of performing arts lessons and classes before she turned four years of age. At the age of three she attended the Clark's Dancing School. If there were no amateur shows or auditions available, Lillian would arrange impromptu gatherings to put Betty on display. Before long, the family moved to the west side of St. Louis and took up residence in the exclusive Forest Park Hotel on Lindell Avenue. There Betty was enrolled in the elite Mary Institute.

As a youth, Betty made many vaudeville (theater combining comedy, song, and dance) performances. She was eventually seen in St. Louis by a talent scout from Hollywood, California. The scout told Lillian to bring Betty to Hollywood. Soon the family was packed into a seven-passenger, custom-built Lincoln automobile that Conn had purchased for the journey. Upon arrival on the West Coast, Betty was enrolled at the Hollywood Professional School. She attended the Ernest Belcher Academy for her dancing lessons and the Albertina Rasch School for her acting classes. When the Great Depression (1929–41) hit, Conn had one of the worst professions in the country, as a stockbroker. However, he found a way to keep enough funds available for Betty to remain in Hollywood. Lillian continued taking her to auditions and parading her before casting directors. She transported her to beauty contests and to appear in theater shows until Betty answered a chorus call at Fox Studios for a film called *Let's Go Places*. Since the minimum age for chorus work was fifteen, Lillian signed false identification papers so that thirteen-year-old Betty was hired.

When Betty's true age was discovered by Fox, she was fired. Lillian immediately drove Betty over to the casting offices of Goldwyn-United Artists. Producer Samuel Goldwyn (c. 1879–1974) signed Betty to a contract, and her first job was to sing the opening line in the first scene of the 1930 musical "Whoopee!" Bit parts continued for the next three years until Betty finally landed a featured spot in the RKO musical *The Gay Divorcee* in 1934. RKO signed her to a second contract and dyed her hair platinum blond. However, Betty continued to seesaw between bit parts and leads. She began a series of

Jane Russell

Unlike Betty Grable, who enjoyed an established Hollywood career by the time World War II (1939–45) erupted, Jane Russell (1921–) largely launched her entertainment career by appealing to servicemen at home and abroad during the war. Businessman and Hollywood producer Howard Hughes (1905–1976) discovered the young actress when casting for his western film, *The Outlaw*, in 1940. The thin plot was centered on the outlaw legend Billy the Kid (1859–1881), but Russell's curvaceous figure was clearly the focus of the film. *The Outlaw* began under the direction of Howard Hawks, but he was soon replaced by Hughes, who had never directed a film but knew what he wanted to see. Because of his inexperience, each scene took thirty or forty takes and one scene took more than one hundred. The entire film required nine months instead of the customary six to eight weeks to shoot. When the picture was finally finished, Russell began posing for publicity stills. Hughes used the photographs to further draw attention to Russell and her physical features.

Jane Russell.

The Outlaw would launch Russell's career as a sex symbol at a time when most Hollywood actresses' roles were rather campus-themed films that identified her for years to come as the wholesome, vivacious, all-American coed. RKO dropped their young starlet's contract in the spring of 1937 after her budding romance with former child star Jackie Coogan (1914–1984) became a news item. Betty and Jackie were married in November 1937, shortly after Betty signed a new contract with Paramount Pictures.

The Coogan marriage brought a great deal of attention and some fame, but the couple divorced in 1940.

wholesome and innocent. The film was almost immediately banned by the Motion Picture Association censors because of the controversy over its sexually explicit content. The film tested the limits of public morality at the time. The footage showing Russell's cleavage provided the most crucial issue in the controversy surrounding the film's limited public showing. Although *The Outlaw* was approved in the spring of 1941, Hughes decided not to release it immediately and instructed his publicity agent to promote Russell into a national celebrity. He intended to take advantage of the extended publicity to generate additional interest in the film. The delay over the film's release left Russell in limbo as an actress, but she continued sitting for an endless series of promotional photographs.

The attack on Pearl Harbor, Hawaii, on December 7, 1941, changed the direction of Hughes's publicity campaign. Now it was aimed at the army, navy, and the marines. Russell went out daily to various military posts and posed with planes and tanks, aboard ships, and with servicemen everywhere. One air force outfit called themselves "Russell's Raiders" in her honor. She would also spend hours in the studio posing in front of the camera in bathing suits, negligees, and shorts. The series of photographs soon became pinups that decorated countless war camp walls on the home front and abroad. In one popular pinup, Russell is reclining suggestively on a stack of hay with pouting lips and her loose-fitting peasant blouse from *The Outlaw*. A second, and more famous, pinup depicts Russell in her peasant blouse with the right shoulder strap slipped down, sitting in a pile of hay that looks as if it had recently been rolled in. Russell's early career was built on barracks' walls during World War II. After the war, *The Outlaw* was released nationally in 1946 and Russell went on to a successful Hollywood career.

Betty Grable was now becoming known to the world on her own, and Paramount began giving her leading roles. A run on the Broadway stage in the 1939 musical hit *DuBarry Was a Lady* landed Grable on the cover of *Life* magazine and made her a household name. Grable signed with Twentieth-Century Fox in 1940, and it was there that she received her big break as female lead in *Down Argentine Way* (1940). Her fan mail was enormous and she rapidly became the hottest property on the Twentieth-Century Fox lot. Grable's stardom came through musical comedies, but it was her "million-dollar legs" that would make her the pinup girl of all pinup girls during World War II.

Wartime pinup queen

The year 1939 was a golden year for Hollywood, with big stars lighting up the silver screen. In Europe, things were growing darker as German forces, led by dictator Adolf Hitler (1889–1945), invaded Poland. The war came earlier to Hollywood than to the rest of America because of the large number of British entertainers working there. When Britain declared war on Germany in September 1939, many returned almost immediately to England. Others delayed their departure to finish films. They then answered the call to respond as members of the British Commonwealth to do their duty for king and country. It would not be until December 1941 that World War II would shatter the calm in Hollywood for American entertainers.

America's declaration of war in 1941 after the Japanese bombing of Pearl Harbor, Hawaii, changed Hollywood's emphasis. Many male performers enlisted in the military, and those left behind looked for ways they could contribute on the home front. Millions of dollars were raised by war bond rallies, and Grable took part in many of them. When the Hollywood Canteen opened on October 3, 1942, Grable performed and then joined other stars in dancing with the young soldiers before they headed off to war. For those soldiers not fortunate enough to have danced with Grable at the Canteen, a substitute phenomenon was about to be born.

The pinup picture of Betty Grable taken by photographer Frank Powolney was copied an estimated five million times and would be owned by one out of every five U.S. servicemen during the war. It was the first, and certainly the best-known, pinup of World War II. The renowned poster had her in a swimsuit, looking back over her shoulder with a mischievous smile. It proved inspirational to those in the middle of war. Other stars soon produced pinups, but Grable was without question the most popular. Hollywood had other glamour queens during the war and loved to give them labels. "The Girl With the Peek-a-Boo Bangs" (Veronica Lake [1919–1973]),

"The Sweater Girl" (Lana Turner [1921–1995]), "The Oomph Girl" (Ann Sheridan [1915–1967]), and "The Sarong" (**Dorothy Lamour** [1914–1996; see entry]) were all popular. Their photographs would adorn barracks walls, smile from foot lockers, and, in pocket size, be carried into battle. Hand-painted reproductions of the same popular photographs would decorate both the inside and the outside of bombers, boats, and Jeeps. By November 1943 it was announced that Betty Grable ranked first in photo requests by military personnel, with Teresa Wright second, and Rita Hayworth third. Fox insured Grable's legs for a million dollars with Lloyd's of London, creating a great deal more publicity.

Before beginning work on the film *Coney Island* (1943), Grable participated in a war bond drive throughout most of the western states. During filming she captained the "Comedians'" football team, which played for war charities at the Los Angeles Coliseum. They played against the "Leading Men," captained by Rita Hayworth. Grable also took her turn visiting hospital wards to help wounded servicemen forget their troubles. Her famous legs made another wartime contribution during a nationwide bond drive in Pulaski, Virginia. A pair of nylon stockings she had worn were sold, with a certificate of authenticity, to the highest bidder for $110,000.

All of Grable's films were exercises in wartime escapism, and in 1943 she made a major leap in popularity from the number eight to the number one female star of the times. Grable married band leader Harry James (1916–1983) that summer and they had two daughters. With her pinup success and continuing lead in lavish musicals, Grable became the highest-paid star in Hollywood and one of the wealthiest women in America. Grable was variously described as "the gal with the gorgeous gams," "the girl with the million-dollar legs," or the girl with "the limbs that launched a thousand sighs." She did not mind at all, as she and her contemporaries in Hollywood took their wartime role very seriously.

Professional pursuits

Grable's career gradually declined after the war ended. By the mid-1950s musicals were no longer popular and television was becoming common in every household. Grable's final film was released in 1955. She then left Hollywood to concentrate on stage and nightclub work. Her most notable tour was in the Broadway musical *Hello Dolly* in 1967. She and Harry James divorced in 1965. Grable continued her lifetime work of entertaining until her death from cancer on July 2, 1973.

For More Information

Books

Hoopes, Roy. *When the Stars Went to War: Hollywood and World War II.* New York: Random House, 1994.

Russell, Jane. *My Path and My Detours.* New York: Franklin Watts, 1985.

Warren, Doug. *Betty Grable: The Reluctant Movie Queen.* New York: St. Martin's Press, 1974.

Web sites

"Betty Grable." *The Roger Richman Agency, Inc.* http://www.hollywoodlegends.com/betty-grable.html (accessed on July 22, 2004).

"Betty Grable." *St. Louis Walk of Fame.* http://www.stlouiswalkoffame.org/inductees/betty-grable.html (accessed on July 22, 2004).

Florence Hall

Born August 1888
Died 1952

Director of Women's Land Army,
home economist

Florence Hall.
National Archives.

In April 1943 the U.S. Department of Agriculture (USDA) announced the appointment of home economist Florence Hall as chief of the Women's Land Army (WLA). The goal of the WLA was to recruit and organize a large number of women to provide farm labor in place of the many farmers and hired hands who had joined the military or left home to take a job in a defense plant.

Hall had been serving as a senior home economist in the Extension Service of the U.S. Department of Agriculture. The Extension Service, in cooperation with state and county government extension services, provided educational services covering all aspects of farming and homemaking on the farm. Hall drew on her experience to skillfully and quickly begin a nationwide recruitment campaign for the WLA. Hall also oversaw and coordinated efforts by WLA supervisors at the local and state levels. She ably communicated to agricultural communities that women could assume most all farm responsibilities and therefore should be hired to help alleviate the wartime farm labor shortage.

Early years

Florence Louise Hall, born in August 1888, was raised in Port Austin, Michigan. Her father, James A. Hall, although a lawyer and banker by profession, owned a nearby farm on which he raised livestock. As a youngster, Florence eagerly enjoyed time at the farm. She learned to ride a horse and milk a cow as well as any rural farm girl. Florence attended college at Michigan State Agricultural College. She graduated in 1909 with a Bachelor of Science degree in home economics.

Following graduation, Florence Hall taught high school mathematics in Lansing, Michigan. At the age of twenty-nine, Hall entered public service for the first time as a home demonstration agricultural agent for Allegheny County, Pennsylvania. Practically applying the knowledge gained during her college years, Hall instructed rural homemakers how to deal with the shortages experienced in World War I (1914–18). She energetically demonstrated how to prepare meatless recipes, the art of canning, and the repair of clothing. Dedicated to her work, Hall related well to the rural wives.

Move to Washington, D.C.

In 1922 Hall joined the Bureau of Dairy Industry within the USDA and moved to her home base in Washington, D.C. She traveled extensively throughout the United States speaking to farming groups, women's organizations, and consumer groups. In 1928 Hall was named as the department's Field Extension agent for the Northeastern United States, from Maine south to West Virginia. Extension agents worked within the USDA's Extension Service Department.

The USDA, quoted in *Current Biography* (1943), had this to say of Hall's job performance: "She has always been greatly absorbed in her work, which has taken her into hundreds of rural homes, talking to groups of home demonstration clubs, always vitally interested in their problems of home furnishing, feeding the family, and planning their wardrobes. She likes to try out the practices recommended in her own home and on her own clothes. It is safe to say that thousands of these farm women feel that they know her personally, and the local home demonstration agents feel that her enthusiasm and practical way of looking at any problem gives them a new lease on their jobs. She is always a popular speaker at farm and home weeks and other big gatherings of farm people, because of her radiant friendliness and her logical, practical way of looking at things."

Despite her close ties to rural America, Hall maintained her home in the heart of Washington, D.C., at an apartment on 16th and Irving Streets, NW. She enjoyed furnishing her home with antiques. Photographs of her living room occasionally showed up in home economist publications.

Women's Land Army

When World War II (1939–45) began for the United States in December 1941, Hall was a proven leader in the Extension Service. By mid-1942, as the farm labor shortage grew, state and local agencies and private groups began to recruit nontraditional workers, including large numbers of women, to bring in the crops. Based on America's "farmerettes" of World War I and women's land armies already functioning in several countries, including Great Britain and Canada, equivalents of women's land armies were organized in the United States, particularly in the Northeast—Volunteer Land Corps of Vermont, Connecticut Land Army, Women's Emergency Farm Service in Maine—and on the West Coast in California and Oregon. Hall kept in close contact with the leaders and was informed of the various groups' activities.

USDA secretary Claude R. Wickard was still reluctant to put women into the fields. Nevertheless, in December 1942 Meredith L. Wilson, director of the Extension Service and charged with drawing plans to meet the farm labor crisis, appointed a three-person committee to study the feasibility of nonfarm women being recruited to work on the farms. The committee consisted of three home economists, Mary A. Rokahr, Grace E. Frysinger, and Hall. By mid-April 1943, WLA was created with Hall at its head. For WLA service Hall was to recruit, organize, and utilize nonfarm women for most types of farm work. WLA women would serve as an emergency wartime farm labor force. Hall's lifestyle, which included both urban and rural aspects, made her a perfect choice to recruit urban women.

Florence Hall, left, and Mabel Mack, supervisor of the Oregon division of the WLA, visit an Oregon peach harvesting operation.
Oregon State University Archives, [P120:2765]. Reproduced by permission.

By overseeing cooperation between the USDA Extension Service, state agricultural colleges, state and county extension agents, and the U.S. Employment Service that recruited in cities, Hall was able to place 250,000 women on farms within months for the 1943 crop season. Hall stressed that the women needed to be strong, possess dexterity, speed, accuracy, and patriotism; however, they needed no experience. Those women expecting to participate year-round would be given several weeks' training at a college to learn farming techniques. Those who would work only temporarily would be trained on the job. Hall understood the need to quickly bring as many women as possible into farm labor. Women were to be paid at the prevailing wage rate for the area in which they worked.

Hall became the chief spokesperson for WLA. She traveled extensively throughout the country on inspection trips to farms, training centers, and camps established to house women workers. She spoke to and coordinated activities with women's volunteer organizations such as the American Women's

Rescuing Crops

By late 1942 there was an acute shortage of labor on America's farms. Between 1940 and 1945, roughly six million farmers and farm workers left the land for more lucrative jobs in defense plants or for the military. Farm women stepped in to keep their farms running while their husbands, fathers, and brothers were away. Although they quickly proved they could handle farm responsibilities, many additional hands were required to tend and harvest crops.

Realizing the burgeoning labor difficulties, the USDA scrambled to locate new sources of farm labor. Approximately 230,000 foreign workers were brought into the United States and 265,000 prisoners of war were used. Eight thousand servicemen received furloughs to plant and harvest, and roughly 26,000 detained Americans of Japanese descent were granted furloughs from their relocation camps for agricultural work. The largest number of workers came from two groups, the Victory Farm Volunteers (VFV), aimed at teenagers, and women.

VFV, 2.5 million teenagers strong, worked the farms in the summertime and when released from school in the fall to aid in the harvest. Women made up the single largest group that stepped forward to "rescue" the crops. In April 1943 the USDA established the Women's Land Army (WLA), which actively and successfully recruited nonfarm women, those not previously involved in any farm labor, for temporary and permanent agricultural work. Between 1943 and 1945 approximately 1.5 million nonfarm women joined WLA. Overall, the USDA estimated three million women—WLA members, women who were hired directly by farmers, and farm wives, daughters, mothers, and grandmothers—plowed, planted, tended, harvested, and preserved a vital portion of the nation's agricultural bounty.

Volunteer Services, YWCA, and the General Federation of Business and Professional Women's Clubs, all of which helped WLA recruit and train. Hall oversaw articles and materials released to the press. Both newspapers and popular magazines jumped on the WLA bandwagon and reported in glowing terms the accomplishments of WLA. One magazine, *Independent Woman,* official publication of the General Federation, even urged workers to plan their vacations around the crop seasons.

In fall 1943 Hall created the *Women's Land Army Newsletter.* It was primarily a newsletter for WLA staff. She provided information about the nationwide program, gave encouragement to WLA supervisors, tips on recruitment and for publicity, and encouraged an open channel of communication between the states to Washington, D.C. Hall also included in the newsletter quotes from farmers praising the exemplary job WLA workers were doing. When WLA was just being established, one of Hall's major challenges had been to convince farmers to allow women onto the farms. The South proved an especially difficult region as fieldwork had long been associated only with black Americans, and because of this Southern whites protested the use of white women in the fields.

In early 1944 the USDA estimated eight hundred thousand women would be needed in agricultural work. The 1944 recruitment pamphlets reported that WLA wages averaged between twenty-five and fifty dollars a month depending on the region of the country. Room and board was furnished. Hourly rates for temporary workers were between twenty-five and fifty cents. Hall's successful recruitment and coordination efforts continued on through the 1945 crop season as did her coordination efforts with WLA supervisors in the states.

On December 10, 1945, Hall issued her last *Women's Land Army Newsletter*. Over the previous two and a half years, women from all vocations had joined the WLA—many university students, housewives, secretaries, clerks, entertainers, bookkeepers, artists, teachers, editors, and government employees. In all, some 1.5 million nonfarm women entered the farm labor force. Some left their jobs to stay on farms year-round while others spent their vacation weeks or weekends. Most all joined out of a patriotic duty to aid in the war effort.

A job well done

Hall's army raised and harvested vegetables in New England, strawberries in Connecticut, fruits in Maine; labored in the cornfields of the Midwest, onion fields of Michigan, peach orchards in Ohio; worked the wheat fields of North Dakota; picked cotton in the South; dug potatoes in Colorado; and harvested fruits, nuts, and vegetables on the West Coast. They drove tractors, milked cows, cared for livestock, tended hens, kept production records, and established canning centers. Wartime food production was kept on track; therefore, food was more available for those on the home front, for combat forces, and for European allies. Hall had made contributions to U.S. agriculture through her entire career. In her last WLA newsletter she stated being director of WLA had indeed been "an enriching experience." Hall died in 1952 at the age of sixty-four.

Although history frequently praises and tells the story of women who worked in the war industries, it largely forgot the wartime women farm workers and the women who led them. Only at the end of the twentieth century and start of the twenty-first century have articles and books appeared telling the story of those women who came to the rescue of U.S. farms during World War II.

For More Information

Books

Block, Maxine, ed. "Hall, Florence (Louise)." In *Current Biography.* New York: H. W. Wilson, 1943.

Carpenter, Stephanie A. *On the Farm Front: The Women's Land Army in World War II.* DeKalb, IL: Northern Illinois University Press, 2003.

Periodicals

Litoff, Judy B., and David C. Smith. "'To the Rescue of the Crops': The Women's Land Army During World War II." *Prologue* (winter 1993): pp. 347–61.

Oveta Culp Hobby

Born January 19, 1905
Killeen, Texas
Died August 16, 1995
Houston, Texas

Director of the Women's Army Corps

Oveta Culp Hobby was an attorney and a journalist who became director of the Women's Army Auxiliary Corps (WAAC). On July 1, 1943, WAAC was given full military status, making it part of the U.S. Army. The unit was renamed Women's Army Corps (WAC) and Hobby became the first female commanding officer in the U.S. Army. She was commissioned a WAC colonel in 1943 and remained as director until July 1945. In January of that year, Hobby received the military's Distinguished Service Medal for outstanding service to her country during World War II (1939–45).

President Dwight D. Eisenhower (1890–1969; served 1953–61) called Hobby back to Washington, D.C., in 1953. Eisenhower appointed her as administrator of the Federal Security Agency. Later that year her appointment was elevated to a presidential cabinet position. Hobby became the first secretary of the newly created Department of Health, Education, and Welfare (HEW) and was the only woman in the Cabinet. Only the second female Cabinet member in American history (the first was Frances Perkins, who served as secretary of labor from 1933 to 1945 under President **Franklin D. Roosevelt**

"(Women) are carrying on the glorious tradition of American womanhood. They are making history! This is a war which recognizes no distinctions between men and women."

Oveta Culp Hobby.
© *Bettmann/Corbis.*
Reproduced by permission.

[1882–1945; served 1933–45; see entry]), Hobby remained in her position at HEW until her return to the Houston *Post* newspaper in 1955. She would eventually chair the newspaper's board.

In the beginning

Oveta Culp was born on January 19, 1905, the second of seven children born to Emma Elizabeth Hoover and Ike W. Culp in Killeen, Texas. She learned her love for the law and the workings of government from her father, who was an attorney and state legislator. From her mother, Oveta learned the importance of community service at an early age. She received her education at the Mary Hardin Baylor College for Women in Texas and from the University of Texas Law School, where she earned her degree in 1925.

After graduation, Oveta served as parliamentarian (expert in legislative rules and procedures) for the Texas House of Representatives until 1931. She accepted a post as assistant to the city attorney of Houston, Texas. There she resumed her friendship with a longtime family friend, William Pettus Hobby (1878–1964).

On February 23, 1931, Oveta Culp married William Hobby, former governor of Texas and the publisher of the Houston *Post*. Oveta was twenty-six while William was fifty-three. The couple had two children. During their early years of marriage, Oveta began working on a book based on her experiences in the legislature. The title was *Mr. Chairman* and, upon publication in 1936, it immediately won acceptance as a handbook on parliamentary law. The Hobbys bought the *Post* newspaper and worked together to pay off the large debt. Oveta learned about publishing and was employed as book editor, assistant editor, and executive vice president. She would eventually become president, editor, and ultimately chairman of the board. She helped run the family-owned business that had expanded to include broadcasting by the early 1940s.

World War II

In 1941 Oveta Culp Hobby was in Washington, D.C., on Federal Communications Commission business. While there, she was asked to head the women's division of the War

Women's Army Corps

With the surprise Japanese bombing of Pearl Harbor, Hawaii, on December 7, 1941, the manpower needs of the U.S. military increased dramatically. The United States was going to fight in both Europe and the Pacific. Some military leaders believed women should take over some of the soldiers' duties on the home front to free the men for combat roles. The Women's Army Auxiliary Corps (WAAC) was formed in May 1942 so that women could serve as typists, file clerks, telephone switchboard operators, bookkeepers, cooks and bakers, radio operators, and drivers of military vehicles, among many other activities. Enrollment was open to women between the ages of twenty-one and forty-four. Some thirty-five thousand women applied for the 440 positions in the first WAAC class to begin officers' training in July 1942. The corps was not considered a part of the regular army until July 1943, when it was converted to the Women's Army Corps (WAC). By then, women had gained greater acceptance and the demand for their services in the military was expanding to include overseas roles. By the end of the war in Europe in June 1945, some 150,000 women had served. While most served on the home front, some 7,600 WACs served in Europe and 5,500 had been stationed in the Southwest Pacific. Another 400 were sent to the China-Burma-India theater. Medals and citations for outstanding military service were presented to 657 WACs. Given their valuable contributions to the war effort, Congress made the WACs a permanent part of the U.S. Army on June 12, 1948.

Department's Bureau of Public Relations. On September 15, 1940, Congress had voted for a compulsory military service and the United States had its first peacetime draft. The War Department was now receiving up to ten thousand letters a day from women, many asking what they could do to serve their country. Hobby was directed to draw up an organizational chart with recommendations on ways women could serve.

Hobby traveled to Europe to study the British and French women's armies for their strengths and weaknesses, while preparing a plan for the United States. She was heading home to Houston, by way of Chicago, Illinois, where she had a speaking engagement, when the surprise Japanese attack on Pearl Harbor, Hawaii, occurred on December 7, 1941.

Hobby immediately returned to Washington, where she met with Secretary of War **Henry L. Stimson** (1867–1950; see entry). He assigned her the task of finding out which regular jobs in the army women could do that would require very little special training. General George C. Marshall (1880–1959) asked her to testify to Congress on the plan for a women's army, and she herself was asked to command that army. When the Women's Army Auxiliary Corps (WAAC) was created on May 14, 1942, Hobby was appointed director with the rank of colonel. Director Hobby found she was traveling constantly in order to speak to large groups of Americans on the radical subject of enlisting volunteer women into the army. The nation was not necessarily ready for this new direction.

Congress had stopped short of making the women's corps an integral part of the army, so the department soon found itself without much power. Because commanding officers were not comfortable with the thought of women soldiers, women were placed in separate units from men. Obstacles to women in the service were everywhere. For example, army engineers insisted that they would work only for the regular army, and so Hobby and her WAAC staff found themselves forced to draw their own barracks' plans. In addition, the comptroller general's office decreed it could not pay the women physicians of the WAAC because they were authorized only to pay persons in military service. Stimson had to ask Congress for a special act to enable Hobby to pay WAAC physicians. But the war, and particularly the attack on Pearl Harbor, forced a change in American thinking. The growing manpower shortage on the home front caused industry to encourage female worker participation in every part of the war effort. The United States needed these women in order to win the war. On all fronts women had proven themselves capable.

In October 1942, First Lady **Eleanor Roosevelt** (1884–1962; see entry) and Colonel Oveta Culp Hobby, as commander of the WAAC, traveled to England to learn about women in the British military. They made a point of visiting the American women pilots who had recently arrived in Europe to fly for the British Royal Air Force. For years the U.S. government had been debating what to do with the organization of women in the service. The question always seemed to focus on the advantages and disadvantages of placing them

Oveta Culp Hobby, head of the WAAC (Women's Army Auxiliary Corps), takes a tour of inspection in London, England, on November 10, 1942. Hobby became the first female commanding officer in the U.S. Army and received the Distinguished Service Medal for outstanding service to her country during World War II. *© Bettmann/Corbis. Reproduced by permission.*

actually in the military and America's readiness to accept women into combat. Several plans included combining the Women's Auxiliary Ferrying Squadron (WAFS) and later the Women's Flying Training Detachment (WFTD) under the leadership of Colonel Hobby at WAAC headquarters. Hobby heartily approved of commissioning women pilots into her organization. The subject was hotly debated on many levels, and the combined women's pilot groups eventually became the Women's Airforce Service Pilots (WASPs). Congress disbanded them before a final decision was ever made about their organization.

The WAAC was made a part of the regular army on July 1, 1943, and renamed Women's Army Corps (WAC). When the corps first organized, Congress hesitantly agreed that women could perform perhaps fifty-four army jobs. By the time Hobby had completed her command in 1945, women filled two hundred and thirty-nine types of jobs. Under her direction, the WAC grew to a maximum strength of about one hundred thousand during the war. In January 1945 Hobby became the first woman to receive the military's Distinguished Service Medal for outstanding service to her country during World War II. Laying aside her colonel's uniform, Hobby returned to Texas to resume her career in journalism.

Back to Washington

President Eisenhower called Hobby back to Washington, D.C., in 1953. Once again she was asked by her nation to organize a new branch of the federal government. Hobby was the first secretary of the newly created Department of Health, Education, and Welfare (HEW), and she was the only woman in the Cabinet. It was a massive and complex department held together by the common thread of family service.

Hobby resigned from her position at HEW in 1955 and returned to Houston to care for her ailing husband. She was the postwar publisher of the Houston *Post* and became chairman of the board of directors of the newly organized Bank of Texas. Always active in Texas Republican politics, Hobby was appointed to the National Advisory Commission on Selective Service by Democratic president Lyndon B. Johnson (1908–1973; served 1963–69). In 1966 she flew to Vietnam as a member of the HEW Vietnam Health Education Task Force to evaluate the situation. Hobby held many honors in her lifetime, but the most meaningful to her was the naming of the library in her hometown of Killeen, Texas. President Johnson was present to dedicate the library at Central Texas College in Hobby's honor. Oveta Culp Hobby was named to the Texas Women's Hall of Fame in 1984. She died in Houston on August 16, 1995.

For More Information

Books

Cott, Nancy F., ed. *No Small Courage: A History of Women in the United States.* New York: Oxford University Press, 2000.

Keil, Sally Van Wagenen. *Those Wonderful Women in Their Flying Machines.* New York: Four Directions Press, 1979.

Read, Phyllis J., and Bernard L. Witlieb. *The Book of Women's Firsts: Breakthrough Achievements of Almost One Thousand American Women.* New York: Random House, 1992.

Verges, Marianne. *On Silver Wings.* New York: Ballantine Books, 1991.

Web sites

"Oveta Culp Hobby." *Cabinet Officials.* http://www.ssa.gov/history/hobby.html (accessed on July 22, 2004).

"Oveta Culp Hobby." *The Texas State Historical Association.* http://www.tsha.utexas.edu/handbook/online/articles/view/HH/fho86.html (accessed on July 22, 2004).

Harold Ickes

Born March 15, 1874
Hollidaysburg, Pennsylvania
Died February 3, 1952
Olney, Maryland

Public administrator

"I have to be consulted before anyone can make any decision on an oil matter. . . . Just how the oil people will take this order I do not know. I suspect that some will like it and some won't."

In May 1941 President **Franklin D. Roosevelt** (1882–1945; served 1933–45; see entry) designated his trusted adviser, Secretary of the Interior Harold Ickes, to be the national coordinator for ensuring the military and home front had adequate gasoline and oil in the event the United States entered the war in Europe. The United States did indeed enter the war less than seven months later. Ickes carried out this important responsibility throughout the war years.

Ickes, known for his crusty and combative personality, promoted the orderly development of the nation's rich natural resources throughout his career, including his time as wartime petroleum administrator during World War II (1939–45). Ickes served as secretary of the interior for thirteen years, from 1933 to 1946, longer than anyone else in U.S. history.

A strict household

The second of seven children, Harold LeClair Ickes was born on March 15, 1874, in Hollidaysburg, Pennsylvania. He grew up in the town of Altoona, located in the rolling

Pennsylvania forested farmland, home of a largely Scotch-Irish population. He acquired a love of nature and the outdoors early in life. The Ickes family had lived in the region since before the American Revolution (1775–83). At one time the family had been large landowners and Harold's grandfather served in the state legislature. However, by the time Harold was born, family fortunes had declined and the family struggled to make ends meet. His father, Jesse Boone Williams Ickes, operated a tobacco store, and his mother, Matilda "Mattie" McClune Ickes, was a homemaker.

A devout Presbyterian, Mattie was a strict disciplinarian. She would allow only religious hymns sung and religious books read on Sundays. She did not allow her children to play or whistle or even walk in the sunshine on the Sabbath. Mattie paid particular attention to young Harold, who showed an unusually strong work ethic and a strong drive to succeed. In response, throughout his life Harold would both admire her in his memories and resent her for the strict religious codes she enforced.

In 1890 when Harold was only sixteen years old, Mattie died of pneumonia. It was a devastating loss to the teen. Harold and a sister went to live in the Chicago suburb of Englewood with an aunt and a very demanding uncle. With little support from his father, Harold worked long hours in his uncle's drugstore while attending high school. On a typical day, Harold would open the store at 6:30 A.M., go to school for the day, and return in the afternoon to work until 10:00 P.M. Despite these long hours, Harold excelled in schoolwork. He was able to combine his junior and senior years and graduated with honors in 1892. In addition, he was president of his senior class.

A Chicago lawyer

Following completion of high school, Harold Ickes moved into Chicago, where he remained for the next forty years. After graduating from the University of Chicago in 1897, Ickes was hired as a newspaper reporter for the Chicago *Tribune* and Chicago *Record*. Through his news gathering, Ickes became interested in the progressive reform movement. The political movement believed in using governmental powers to solve national social and economic problems. Through his political activities, he met businessman and city planner Frederic Delano, uncle of young Franklin Delano Roosevelt.

After graduating from the University of Chicago's law school in 1907, Ickes established a private practice in the city. During the 1920s he fought the power of big business in defending the rights of the common people, such as representing the legal interests of women industrial workers. He was also director of the Chicago branch of the National Association for the Advancement of Colored People (NAACP), promoting greater economic opportunity for black Americans.

New Dealer

After Ickes campaigned vigorously for Roosevelt in the 1932 presidential elections, the newly elected president rewarded him with the position of secretary of the interior. In his new position, Ickes was committed to the orderly development of the nation's natural resources through careful governmental planning. He identified conservation projects for the newly created Civilian Conservation Corps (CCC) and directed the Public Works Administration (PWA), both New Deal agencies. The New Deal referred to a collection of programs created by President Roosevelt to bring relief and recovery to citizens suffering under the worst U.S. economic crisis in history, the Great Depression (1929–41). Through the PWA, Ickes personally guided the allocation of six billion dollars of federal funds to public works projects including construction of large dams, tunnels, hospitals, schools, highways, post offices, and other public structures. The PWA completed nineteen thousand projects, including the Hoover Dam on the Colorado River, Grand Coulee Dam on the Columbia River, and many other large water and power projects. The projects provided desperately needed jobs. Through the CCC, which provided jobs for unemployed young men, Ickes pursued natural resources conservation programs such as soil conservation projects and reforestation of millions of acres of forestland that had been burned or cut. Despite his hard work, Ickes did not attract a strong public following due to his harsh personality shaped by his strict, disciplined childhood.

William Jeffers—Rubber Coordinator

Like the oil resources that Secretary of the Interior Harold Ickes was appointed to coordinate production and use of during World War II (1939–45), rubber was another critical raw material needed for the war. However, 90 percent of the U.S. sources for rubber were disrupted by Japanese military expansion in Southeast Asia and the Western Pacific by the early 1940s. The dire need to coordinate the replacement of those sources fell to railroad executive William M. Jeffers (1876–1953).

Jeffers was one of nine children born to William and Elizabeth Gannon Jeffers in North Platte, Nebraska, in January 1876. His father, an Irish immigrant, was a laborer for Union Pacific Railroad. Young William began working for Union Pacific at fourteen years of age. Through the next forty-seven years, Jeffers rose through the ranks to become president of Union Pacific in 1937. Under his leadership, Union Pacific became one of the most financially successful railroads in the United States. Known for his hard-driving, no-nonsense management style, Jeffers was asked by the Roosevelt administration in September 1942 to be the national rubber director. He was given the responsibility to bring order to the rubber industry and guarantee a reliable supply for the war effort. Jeffers immediately demanded gas rationing to conserve the existing rubber supply and then promoted the use of rayon for the development of synthetic rubber. The government spent seventy million dollars to construct fifty-one plants for lease to rubber companies. By 1944 more than eight hundred thousand tons of synthetic rubber was being produced a year. Synthetic rubber production amounted to 87 percent of the rubber used for the war. The development of the synthetic rubber capacities is considered one of the biggest home front achievements in World War II. Jeffers died in Pasadena, California, in March 1953.

Ickes was quick to speak out, and act, on controversial social issues. For example, in the interest of promoting civil rights causes, Ickes ended racial segregation in his department, ensured that blacks received a fair share of construction jobs in the projects funded by the Interior Department, and promoted the appointment of the first black federal judge, William Hastie (1904–1976), on March 26, 1937. Ickes also personally arranged for the internationally famous black singer Marian Anderson (1897–1993) to sing at the Lincoln Memorial on Easter Sunday in 1939 in front of thousands in an open-air concert when she was denied use of a private concert hall in Washington, D.C.

In the late 1930s, Ickes was the first in the Roosevelt administration to publicly speak out against the popular aviator Charles Lindbergh's (1902–1974) isolationist (opposition to war and formal international relations) views. He also aggressively spoke out against military dictatorships growing in Germany and Italy. He would also later speak out against Roosevelt's internment (imprisonment) of Japanese Americans after the bombing of Pearl Harbor, Hawaii, by the Japanese in 1941.

Importance of oil in war

Nothing is more important in supporting military machinery in a war than having sufficient gasoline and oil, particularly when mechanized warfare had come of age by the early twentieth century. To build and maintain adequate armed services, the home front also needed a reliable supply of petroleum, particularly the war industries.

Ickes had always been a trusted adviser of the president. With war becoming increasingly imminent, Roosevelt was very concerned about the nation's petroleum fuel reserves. Prior to 1941 the federal government had little regulation over the petroleum industry, limited only to some aspects of the interstate trade of petroleum. This limited control had existed only since 1933, as part of Roosevelt's New Deal programs to rescue the nation from the economic problems of the Great Depression. During the late 1930s, several federal agencies tackled the issues of oil conservation and the discovery of new sources. Among these were the Bureau of Mines, Petroleum Conservation Division, and the U.S. Geological Survey, all overseen by Secretary of the Interior Ickes. In addition to these federal agencies, the various oil-producing states also had public agencies overseeing oil production within their own states.

By early 1941, it was clear that the haphazard system of production, transportation, and use of oil had to be improved. In March the National Resources Planning Board recommended to the president that a single federal authority be designated to coordinate the oil industry on the home front.

Within the next couple of months, fuel crises began developing. A shortage of oil tankers created by using fifty tankers to transport needed war supplies to Great Britain threatened the supply of oil to the growing U.S. war industries. By early May, Ickes and others urged Roosevelt to establish federal regulation of oil supplies. In response, on May 27 Roosevelt declared an unlimited national emergency. On the following day, he designated Ickes the Petroleum Coordinator for National Defense.

Workers struggle to move a large section of pipe across snow as part of the effort to build an emergency oil pipeline during World War II in Glen Moore, Pennsylvania. Harold Ickes was largely responsible for the nation's development of interstate pipelines, which helped avoid a major oil and gasoline shortage during the critical war years.
© Bettmann/Corbis.
Reproduced by permission.

Petroleum coordinator

As petroleum coordinator, Ickes was charged with gathering information on how much petroleum would be needed for the war effort by the military and on the home front, and the supply available. Ickes was also to determine what it would take to increase oil production efficiency.

Through 1941 Ickes guided inventories of the home front capacity for production, transportation, refining, and distribution of oil, and what equipment the oil industry needed to sustain the supply. Based on these inventories, Ickes began developing plans for expanding oil production capabilities to produce high-octane gasoline and for supplying Great Britain and the Soviet Union with petroleum. Of concern was the development of additional crude oil and natural gas reserves, the development of adequate transportation and storage facilities, and an increase in the efficiency of delivering oil to its destinations. Armed with this information, Ickes advised federal and state agencies and the oil industry on what was needed to maintain a steady, adequate supply of petroleum. Ickes was also to advise the Office of Production Management (OPM) concerning possible home front rationing needs to ensure the war industries were receiving adequate petroleum supplies. However, the gas rationing that did occur was designed more for conserving rubber in car tires than conserving gasoline. Ickes also had to coordinate supplies with the various foreign nations relying on U.S. supplies.

Upon the bombing of Pearl Harbor on December 7, 1941, Roosevelt changed Ickes's title to Petroleum Coordinator for War. As the war progressed and intensified through 1942, Roosevelt determined that Ickes needed stronger authority than simply advising the various agencies and industry. Therefore on December 2, 1942, the president established the Petroleum Administration for War with Ickes as its head. Under Ickes's leadership the nation saw no major disruption of oil supplies after some limited shortages in 1942 in the eastern United States.

An active retirement

Following the end of the war and the death of Roosevelt, Ickes resigned as secretary of the interior on February 13, 1946. He was one of the last key players of Roosevelt's administration to leave office. Ickes retired to his farm in Olney, Maryland, outside of Washington, D.C. He maintained an office in Georgetown, adjacent to Washington, D.C., where he wrote various books and magazine articles. Included was the completion of a detailed diary he had kept through his term as secretary of the interior from 1933 to 1946. It was published in three volumes in the early 1950s after his death. Titled

The Secret Diary of Harold L. Ickes, the set provided a unique insider's view of the New Deal and the World War II home front. He also wrote columns on political issues for the New York *Post* and *New Republic* magazine, and a series of articles for the *Saturday Evening Post.* Not surprisingly, his pointed articles tackled controversial issues such as the anticommunist crusade of U.S. senator Joseph McCarthy (1908–1957) in the early 1950s. Ickes also maintained an active speaking schedule. He died at age seventy-eight near his home at Olney, Maryland, on February 3, 1952.

For More Information

Books

Clarke, Jeanne N. *Roosevelt's Warriors: Harold L. Ickes and the New Deal.* Baltimore: Johns Hopkins University Press, 1996.

Ickes, Harold L. *The Secret Diary of Harold L. Ickes: The First Thousand Days, 1933–1936; The Inside Struggle, 1936–1939; The Lowering Clouds, 1939–1941.* 3 vols. New York: Simon & Schuster, 1952–54.

Watkins, T. H. *Righteous Pilgrim: The Life and Times of Harold L. Ickes, 1874–1952.* New York: Henry Holt, 1990.

White, Graham J. *Harold Ickes of the New Deal: His Private Life and Public Career.* Cambridge, MA: Harvard University Press, 1985.

Henry Kaiser

Born May 9, 1882
Sprout Brook, New York
Died August 24, 1967
Honolulu, Hawaii

Industrialist

Henry Kaiser.
The Library of Congress.

Henry Kaiser's imprint on American industry was remarkable. He has been called the "father of modern shipbuilding" and was considered the most powerful businessman in the U.S. West during World War II (1939–45). The concrete he manufactured went to build Pacific military bases, his aluminum into new advanced warplanes, his steel into warships, and the thousands of cargo ships he built carried troops and supplies across the oceans to the European and Pacific war fronts. The electricity generated by the dams he built fueled the West Coast war industries. Kaiser became a favorite of the news media and was considered by many to be the most influential civilian to help America win the war.

A born worker

Henry John Kaiser was born on May 9, 1882, in Sprout Brook, New York. Both of his parents were emigrants from Steinham, Germany. Henry grew up in a family of modest means. His father, Frank, was a shoemaker. His mother, Mary Yops, first worked in a cheese factory and then became a part-time nurse as the family began to grow. Henry, the youngest of four children, had three older sisters. Throughout his life, Henry would always credit his mother for giving him the principles of hard work and determination that led to his business success. Her untimely death at fifty-two years of age in 1899 profoundly affected young Henry and likely inspired his later interest in establishing preventative medicine systems.

Young Henry quit school following the eighth grade at age thirteen. It was not so much to support the family but simply because he was eager to work. His friends described Henry as an energetic, bright individual. He was very outgoing and assertive, yet pleasant. He found a job as a dry goods clerk in the nearby town of Utica. For the next several years through various sales jobs, Henry Kaiser honed his ability to readily sell others on an idea or product. Kaiser's strong combination of charisma and salesmanship made him a very persuasive young man.

Kaiser also became interested in photography and began developing his photography skills while away from the store. The Eastman-Kodak Company, located near Utica, was making major advances in photography during the 1890s inventing smaller cameras including the Brownie model that could be used by the general public and not just professional photographers. Inspired by these developments, Kaiser launched a new career as a photographer by age sixteen. Always ambitious, by 1901 he became part owner of a studio in Lake Placid, New York, and by 1903, after saving several thousand dollars, he opened several photography shops in Florida. He made postcards, promotional photographs for railroads, and portraits. Kaiser enjoyed the annual cycle of working the five summer months in Lake Placid and the remainder of the year in Florida.

A move west

Through a fateful portrait session, Kaiser met his future wife, Bess Fosburgh, in 1906. He soon proposed marriage. However, Bess's father, a wealthy Virginia lumber businessman, challenged Kaiser to gain more stable employment before marrying his daughter. More specifically, he was to go out West, make at least $125 a month, and build a home for his future wife. In response, Kaiser sold his Florida studios and moved to Spokane, Washington. There Kaiser became a very successful traveling salesman for the McGowan Brothers wholesale hardware business. He and Bess married in Boston, Massachusetts, in April 1907 and returned to Spokane, where they had two sons.

During the first decade of the twentieth century, automobiles were just coming into general use. While on his frequent travels as a hardware salesman, Kaiser became increasingly aware of the need for better public streets and roads for the growing number of automobiles. Seeing the business potential, Kaiser left the hardware business in 1909 and joined a cement and gravel company in Spokane to learn the trade. Before long, he began work for a Canadian road construction company. In December 1914 Kaiser took over the company, which was going bankrupt, and quickly rebuilt it. Through the following years, Kaiser gained respect in the construction industry as he built numerous roads in California, Oregon, and Washington. He played a major role in creating the infrastructure (public roads and key facilities) of the West. By 1921 he moved his company headquarters from Vancouver, British Columbia, to Oakland, California. Kaiser enjoyed the economic boom times of the 1920s as new construction nearly doubled in the United States. He established local sand and gravel companies to supply his own road materials. Besides roads, he built various other structures such as dams and levees. He even constructed a highway across Cuba that crossed swamp lands and included five hundred bridges.

Establishing a Washington, D.C., link

With even bigger projects in mind, in 1931 Kaiser joined his company with several others to form Six Companies. They won a government contract to build the Hoover Dam on the Colorado River in southern Nevada. It would be the world's largest dam. Kaiser served as the communication link between the giant company and the federal government. He spent considerable time in Washington, D.C., between 1931 and 1935 gaining knowledge of government contracting processes and making many contacts with administrators of public works

Liberty Ships

Of all the businesses Henry Kaiser founded during his career, he is best known for his World War II (1939–45) shipbuilding yards. In 1941 under the Emergency Ship-building Program, the U.S. Maritime Commission (USMC) began a massive expansion of the merchant marine fleet. A central part of the program was a standard designed cargo ship called a Liberty Ship. Designed for emergency production, President Franklin D. Roosevelt (1882–1945; served 1933–45) referred to them as "ugly duck-lings." At first the USMC planned to con-struct 60 ships for the British, which grew to 112. The first Liberty Ship was com-pleted on September 27, 1941. Over the next year, Kaiser shortened the time of production from 197 days for each ship to 14 days. The record was 4 days, 15 hours, and 30 minutes.

Each of the 441 foot-long ships cost about two million dollars. Each could carry nine thousand tons of cargo inside its hull and airplanes, tanks, or other equipment on its deck. A Liberty Ship could carry 2,840 jeeps, 440 tanks, or 230 million rounds of rifle bullets. A crew of forty-four would sail the ship and some twenty Naval Armed Guards would man the nine large guns, fitted for protection.

Constituting the largest production program for a single type of ship, a total of 2,710 Liberty Ships were built by sixteen shipyards in the United States. Another 119 revised Liberty Ships were also produced. The ships were built in assembly-line fashion, made from parts prefabricated at various other locations. Each ship had 600,000 feet of welded joints. Kaiser's seven yards built 821 ten-ton Liberty Ships and 219 Victory Ships, a slightly improved version of Liberty Ships. Liberty Ships comprised 27 percent of total World War II shipping. Of the 2,710 built, only 200 were lost in action.

The same day a ship was com-pleted, its crew boarded and they set off to sea to join one of hundreds of convoys crossing the Atlantic or Pacific Oceans. The ships were named after prominent deceased Americans, with early American leader Patrick Henry (1736–1799) being the first. Any organization that raised enough money through the sale of war bonds to fund con-struction of a Liberty Ship could provide a name. In 2003 two Liberty Ships survived as public museums.

projects. Kaiser also created Boulder City, Nevada, a planned community to house the Hoover Dam workers and their fami-lies consisting of about five thousand people. It was the first planned city in the United States during the twentieth century. President **Franklin D. Roosevelt** (1882–1945; served 1933–45;

see entry) came to dedicate the Hoover Dam in 1935 near its completion.

After completing the Hoover Dam, Six Companies won more government contracts to build the Bonneville and Grand Coulee Dams in the late 1930s on the Columbia River in Oregon and Washington. It also won the contract to build the San Francisco Bay Bridge connecting the city of San Francisco, California, with the east side of San Francisco Bay. Though Six Companies failed to win the contract to build the Shasta Dam in northern California, Kaiser's own company became the key supplier of cement for the project beginning in 1939. In order to produce the six million barrels of cement required, Kaiser built the world's largest cement plant, Permanente Cement, that year south of San Francisco.

World War II shipyards

Though highly successful and nearing the age of sixty, Kaiser would be further propelled into national prominence with the advent of World War II. As German forces expanded through Western Europe in early 1940, Kaiser became concerned about the limited U.S. industrial capacity, especially for steel and aluminum production. He also believed if the United States were drawn into the war, a great demand for shipping would exist. As a result, Kaiser became outspoken about mobilizing U.S. industry. Mobilization became the key word used to describe converting American industry from peacetime to wartime uses. Through his efforts, he built a close friendship with President Roosevelt.

As the war in Europe expanded, Great Britain looked to the United States for much needed supplies. In December 1940 Kaiser and two partners won a government contract to build thirty cargo ships for the British. For this project he built a large shipyard in Richmond, California, and used workers from the Grand Coulee Dam project. Though he had no previous experience in shipbuilding, his industrial production genius led to national fame. His shipyards were the first to build a ship in separate sections prior to final assembly and to weld steel plates together instead of using rivets. In late 1940 Kaiser also won a government contract from the Defense Plant Corporation to build aluminum plants on the West Coast to

supply aluminum for aircraft manufacturers. More contracts followed in 1941 from the U.S. maritime commission. He built another large shipyard near Portland, Oregon, and established the town of Vanport in 1942 for the workers. A flood would later destroy Vanport in 1948 after the war. In all, Kaiser ran seven shipyards during the war, employing some two hundred thousand workers. Kaiser's shipyards built 1,490 ships, including 1,112 cargo ships and 107 warships. The warships included

The first day of construction of the 10,500 ton freighter named the *Joseph N. Teal,* at Henry Kaiser's shipbuilding yard in Portland, Oregon, on September 25, 1942.
© Bettmann/Corbis.
Reproduced by permission.

50 small aircraft carriers. Kaiser built one-third of the nation's cargo ships for the war.

Kaiser was the subject of hundreds of magazine articles. He was a favorite of media giant Henry R. Luce (1898–1967) of *Time-Life-Fortune*. The media referred to Kaiser as the "Miracle Man" and America's "Number One Industrial Hero." Roosevelt even considered naming Kaiser as his running mate for the 1944 presidential elections. In 1943 when Kaiser established an experimental laboratory to explore various new projects, the public would continually send him new ideas for inventions.

Kaiser, however, was less popular among other industrial leaders. Many disliked his headline notoriety and suspected he was receiving favoritism from Washington because of his close association with the president. Through 1941 other industry leaders opposed some of Kaiser's project proposals, particularly his proposal to build a major steel mill in the West to supply his shipyards. Most steel was produced in the East. However, following the shock of the Japanese bombing of U.S. military installations at Pearl Harbor in Hawaii in December 1941, Kaiser received millions of dollars in government loans to build a large steel mill east of Los Angeles in Fontana. Meanwhile, his Permanente plant produced a large portion of the cement used in the Pacific to construct military installations.

In a public poll conducted near war's end in the spring of 1945, the public listed Kaiser as the U.S. civilian who had done the most to help win the war. A 1946 public poll named Kaiser a strong prospect for U.S. president.

After the war

The sudden death of President Roosevelt in April 1945 broke Kaiser's well-placed connection to Washington. With the war over and Roosevelt gone, Kaiser closed his Washington office. Kaiser could constantly predict future U.S. wants and needs. Back when war production was in full stride in 1943, he began planning for an anticipated postwar economic boom. One idea was to produce inexpensive automobiles. The manufacture of automobiles had been suspended during the war, and he anticipated a large demand afterwards. In 1945 Kaiser joined with Joseph W. Frazer, an automobile industry executive, to form the Kaiser-Frazer Corporation. They purchased the large Willow Run plant outside of Detroit, Michigan, that was no longer needed for war production. Sales of the Kaiser cars were good. By September 1947 the company was manufacturing fifteen thousand cars a month. They produced more than three hundred thousand cars in 1947 and 1948, earning $29 million. However, by late 1948 the big car manufacturers of General Motors (GM), Ford, and Chrysler were catching up, thanks to their larger research and development capabilities. The Kaiser cars steadily lost ground until the mid-1950s, when Kaiser stopped production. By then, this endeavor had lost 123 million dollars.

Kaiser's other industries prospered in the postwar period, including Kaiser Steel and Kaiser Aluminum. Kaiser Aluminum remained one of the top three aluminum producers in the second half of the twentieth century. In 1956 he formed Kaiser Industries to oversee the various companies, and in 1962 Kaiser constructed a new high-rise headquarters office building in Oakland, California. However, Kaiser's industrial domain proved less competitive during the Cold War. The Cold War was an intense political and economic rivalry from 1945 to 1991 between the United States and the Soviet Union falling just short of military conflict. Kaiser never gathered the scientists and engineers needed to keep up with the fast-appearing technological innovations. His leadership gave way to other newly rising West Coast industrial entrepreneurs such as Howard Hughes (1905–1976) of Hughes Aircraft.

Health plan

In 1938 Kaiser had introduced a company health plan and hospital program, the nation's first health maintenance program. It was a prepaid plan for workers at Grand Coulee Dam. The program grew dramatically during the war, covering the thousands of shipyard workers. After the war, it was opened to the general public and became the nation's largest health organization by 1967, with 1.5 million members and nineteen hospitals providing preventive health care. Kaiser also established nursing schools and aided medical education programs. The Kaiser system of partnerships among physicians served as a model for federal health care programs.

Semi-retirement

In 1951 Kaiser's wife, Bess, died after a lengthy illness, and Kaiser married Bess's nurse only weeks later, creating a small scandal. In 1954 he semi-retired to Hawaii, where he built a large resort and cement factory. In 1961 he sold the resort to Hilton for more than twenty-one million dollars. Kaiser also led in the development of the planned community of Hawaii Kai on Oahu. He sponsored radio and television programs, including the popular television series *Maverick*. Kaiser died in Hawaii on August 24, 1967, after a brief illness. Throughout his life, Kaiser had founded more than one hundred companies. In 1986 the 677-foot long USNS *Henry J. Kaiser*, a naval refueling ship, was added to the U.S. Navy's Seventh Fleet. It was converted to a tanker in 1995.

For More Information

Books

Adams, Stephen B. *Mr. Kaiser Goes to Washington: The Rise of a Government Entrepreneur.* Chapel Hill, NC: University of North Carolina Press, 1997.

Foster, Mark S. *Henry J. Kaiser: Builder in the Modern American West.* Austin, TX: University of Texas Press, 1989.

Heiner, Albert P. *Henry J. Kaiser: Western Colossus.* San Francisco, CA: Halo Books, 1981.

Nash, Gerald D. *The American West Transformed: The Impact of the Second World War.* Lincoln, NE: University of Nebraska Press, 1990.

Web sites

The Henry J. Kaiser Family Foundation. http://www.kff.org (accessed on July 22, 2004).

United States Navy. http://www.msc.navy.mil/mpstwo/kaiser.htm (accessed on July 22, 2004).

Fiorello La Guardia

Born December 11, 1882
New York, New York
Died September 20, 1947
Bronx, New York

New York City mayor, national director
of Civilian Defense

A highly successful three-term mayor of New York City from 1933 to 1945, Fiorello La Guardia was director of the nation's civilian defense programs at the beginning of World War II (1939–45) and provided leadership to the nation's largest city throughout the war. He brought organization and rapid growth to such programs as air raid warning systems, scrap metal drives, and Victory gardens. Under his direction more than eight thousand community civil defense organizations, consisting of more than five million volunteers, were loosely linked into a national network within only weeks after the attack on Pearl Harbor.

"Rejoice, be happy, make merry, but please do not use any sound-making device, any siren or horn that would resemble the [civilian defense] alarm in your community."

A worldly start

Fiorello Henry La Guardia was born on December 11, 1882, in New York City. His father, Achille La Guardia, was an army bandmaster and his mother, Irene Coen, a homemaker. After an illness, Achille was discharged from the army and Fiorello was raised in Arizona until at age sixteen, in 1898, he and his mother moved to Budapest, Hungary. At eighteen years of age, Fiorello was selected to a post with the American

Fiorello La Guardia.
© Bettmann/Corbis.
Reproduced by permission.

consular service. While working in continental Europe, he acquired fluency in five languages. Wanting to return to the United States, Fiorello returned to New York. There he obtained work as an interpreter for the U.S. Immigration Service at Ellis Island, where new immigrants arrived from foreign lands. While working at Ellis Island, Fiorello took law courses at New York University Law School. He was admitted to the New York bar (legal association) in 1910.

Fiorello La Guardia had an interest in politics. In 1914 he ran as a Republican candidate for U.S. Congress but lost. Undeterred, he ran again in 1916 and won representing lower Manhattan. With two brief interruptions, La Guardia would serve in Congress until 1932. One interruption came during World War I (1914–18) in 1917, when he and four other congressmen joined the military. La Guardia was stationed in Fogia, Italy, where he flew fighter planes and worked in undercover operations. He ended his service with the rank of a major.

Upon returning from war, he resumed his congressional career and married Thea Almerigiotti in 1919. They had a daughter. However, both his wife and daughter soon died of tuberculosis (an infectious lung disease). The deaths made a major mark on La Guardia, who took up the cause of improving the lives of the poor since tuberculosis thrived in the slums and industrial sweatshops. La Guardia crusaded against big business, the wealthy, and racists.

In Congress, La Guardia joined a group of progressives who favored the use of governmental power to improve the nation's economic and social conditions. He campaigned for industrial regulations and against racist immigration policies. He also supported equal rights for women, child labor laws, and opposed Prohibition (the movement to prohibit the sale and use of alcoholic beverages). He cosponsored the Norris–La Guardia Act of 1932 increasing labor's ability to conduct strikes. The act limited the ability of courts to interfere with strikes, boycotts, or picketing by organized labor.

A popular mayor

In 1929 La Guardia remarried, this time to his longtime secretary Marie Fisher. They would adopt two children.

That same year he ran for mayor of New York but lost to a popular incumbent. Then in 1932 he lost his congressional seat to the Democratic landslide election that brought President **Franklin D. Roosevelt** (1882–1945; served 1933–45; see entry) into office. Political fortunes soon turned again in 1933 when the New York mayor resigned under charges of corruption. La Guardia was able to assemble the support of a coalition of diverse political groups to win the resulting election.

La Guardia entered the mayor's office in January 1934 with the Great Depression (1929–41) still at its worst. More than 230,000 workers were unemployed in New York and almost 20 percent were on relief. In his characteristically flashy manner, La Guardia tackled the lost public confidence in local government in which there was no public housing, few social and health services including old-age pensions and unemployment insurance, and declining public facilities including the city's roads and bridges. La Guardia introduced the use of appointed experts to solve the various problems. The city became transformed through the acquisition of substantial federal funding assistance. Under La Guardia sewer systems were improved; new bridges, tunnels, reservoirs, parks, schools, hospitals, highways, health centers, and public housing built. Also included was construction of La Guardia Airport. He even provided financial assistance for the arts and music. Much of the relief was funded by a new sales tax. Gaining a reputation as an honest and hardworking reformer, La Guardia modernized New York's government with improved city police and fire departments, expanded social welfare services, and clearance of slums.

His popularity and forcefulness made La Guardia a powerful mayor. Short and stout, standing at only 5 feet 2 inches, he was called "The Little Flower," a direct Italian translation of his first name. He made New York a leader in providing for the social welfare of its citizens and shaping federal policies toward cities. La Guardia was elected president of the U.S. Conference of Mayors from 1936 to 1945. In 1939 New York hosted the World's Fair with the theme of the World of Tomorrow. His working relationship with President Roosevelt and his New Deal programs grew very close as he brought home a large amount of federal funds.

A Fast Start for Civilian Defense

Though the target of much criticism while director of the Office of Civilian Defense (OCD), Fiorello La Guardia saw much progress made on home front preparedness for war during his time in that position. By the end of January 1942, only eight months after the OCD was created, some 8,478 local civilian defense councils were established in many towns and cities. There were also 334,666 auxiliary (assisting or providing help) police, 670,673 air raid wardens, and 265,580 medical staff. In all, more than five million volunteers worked in civilian defense. Civilian defense provided a productive avenue for citizens on the home front to contribute to the war effort.

Civilian defense

In spring of 1941 with war approaching, Roosevelt appointed the highly popular and energetic La Guardia the director of the newly established Office of Civilian Defense (OCD). For the next year, La Guardia tried to serve in the OCD position as well as mayor of New York. As OCD director he created a large force of volunteers in all cities and towns to protect citizens and property from the possibilities of air raids or other wartime home front emergencies. OCD was also charged with coordinating scrap metal drives and encouraging conservation of food, such as through the tending of victory gardens by thousands of households. Besides his two important governmental wartime posts and serving as president of the U.S. Conference of Mayors, La Guardia also served as chairman of the Joint United States-Canadian Defense Board. In his civilian defense capacity, La Guardia would regularly attend Cabinet meetings. He also made regular shortwave radio broadcasts to Italy warning Italian citizens of the dangers of German dictator Adolf Hitler (1889–1945). La Guardia became one of the most familiar names in America.

One key responsibili1ty of OCD under La Guardia was distributing important survival information to the public. In 1941 the OCD published *Handbook for Air Raid Wardens*. It also published the *Handbook for First Aid* in cooperation with the American Red Cross. Following the bombing of Pearl Harbor, Hawaii, on December 7, 1941, OCD published *What Can I Do? The Citizens' Handbook for War*. La Guardia also encouraged local civilian defense organizations to publish guides. Two months before Pearl Harbor, a New York civilian defense organization published a handbook titled *The Air Raid Protection (A.R.P.) Organization* and the Queens Civilian Defense Volunteer Office in New York City published a one-page leaflet titled "What to Do in an Air Raid." The Civilian Defense Volunteer Office in

Forest Hills, New York, also published *Block Organizations,* which described how to organize local civilian defense volunteer organizations.

While tackling these diverse tasks, La Guardia came under fire from two directions. Much of the home front did not want to hear about going to war throughout most of 1941. Many New Yorkers thought La Guardia had spread himself too thin and should choose between being the New York City mayor and being OCD national director. As time passed, it became clearer he could not effectively do both. In the fall of 1941 La Guardia barely won reelection as mayor.

In addition, conflicts arose between President Roosevelt and La Guardia over the emphasis of certain programs within the OCD. In an effort to resolve this difference, the president appointed his wife, First Lady **Eleanor Roosevelt** (1884–1962; see entry), as an assistant to La Guardia to address activities that La Guardia did not wish or have time in his busy schedule to personally tackle. While La Guardia focused on air raid warning

New York City Mayor Fiorello La Guardia and First Lady Eleanor Roosevelt make a joint broadcast on September 6, 1941, to urge citizens to organize local civil defense councils.
© *Bettmann/Corbis. Reproduced by permission.*

systems, Eleanor began planning physical fitness centers and the creation of an arts council. Many in the conservative Congress thought this a waste of funding and a distraction from the more immediate war effort. Critics charged that these activities were not a part of the OCD mission to protect communities from air raids. Also, the personalities of La Guardia and Eleanor Roosevelt clashed. La Guardia had an energetic flair for the dramatic while Eleanor had a much quieter and calm manner.

La Guardia and Eleanor did have some effective moments together. On December 8, 1941, the day after the surprise Japanese attack on Pearl Harbor, La Guardia and Eleanor flew to the West Coast. Their intent was to better organize the OCD volunteer program while calming fears among citizens of further attacks.

However, the OCD remained under fire from Congress into 1942. First Eleanor and then La Guardia resigned from OCD in February 1942. La Guardia refocused on his duties as mayor of New York and guided home front activities in that major city. In addition, La Guardia still wanted a larger national war role. He lobbied Roosevelt for an appointment as general in the European theater, but Roosevelt declined. La Guardia was bitterly disappointed.

In 1946 La Guardia chose not to run for a fourth term as New York mayor. He felt that he had achieved most of what he had intended as mayor. La Guardia accepted a position as director of the new United Nations Relief and Rehabilitation Administration to help in postwar recovery in Europe and elsewhere. However, his health was failing owing to his energetic contributions to the home front war effort. He died in the Bronx, New York, on September 20, 1947.

For More Information

Books

Eliott, Lawrence. *Little Flower: The Life and Times of Fiorello La Guardia.* New York: Morrow, 1983.

Kessner, Thomas. *Fiorello H. La Guardia and the Making of Modern New York.* New York: McGraw-Hill, 1989.

Lingeman, Richard R. *Don't You Know There's a War On? The American Home Front, 1941–1945.* New York: G.P. Putnam's Sons, 1970.

Dorothy Lamour

Born December 10, 1914
New Orleans, Louisiana
Died September 22, 1996
Los Angeles, California

Film actress

Dorothy Lamour was a famous Hollywood actress known as "the bond bombshell" because of her volunteer work selling U.S. war bonds during World War II (1939–45). The sale of war bonds became a patriotic way for those on the home front to contribute to the national defense and war effort. It was a unique combination of patriotism and consumerism that sold $185.7 billion in securities (bonds). Over the course of the war, Lamour sold some $300 million of the bonds around the country. Other members of Hollywood's entertainment community used their celebrity status to help sell war bonds, but Lamour was credited with being the first star to offer her services to do so.

The first U.S. Savings Bond was sold to President **Franklin D. Roosevelt** (1882–1945; served 1933–45; see entry) on May 1, 1941. There would be seven war bond drives in the series. On January 3, 1946, the last proceeds from the Victory Bond campaigns were deposited into the U.S. Treasury. Although the initial goal of the war bond campaign was to finance the war, its greatest accomplishment would be the positive boost it had on the morale of home front Americans.

"Newspaper clippings document my whole last [war] bond tour in which I traveled 1,500 miles in nine days, visited 25 cities, and sold $31,439,515 worth of bonds."

Dorothy Lamour.
The Kobal Collection.
Reproduced by permission.

Beauty queen

Mary Leta Dorothy Slaton was born in the charity ward of a New Orleans, Louisiana, hospital on December 10, 1914. Her parents, Carmen Louise La Porte and John Watson Slaton, soon divorced and her mother was briefly married to Clarence Lambour. Her stepfather's name was later adapted to create Dorothy's stage name, Lamour. Dorothy was a beautiful child who grew up to win the Miss New Orleans beauty contest in 1931. She and her mother then moved to Chicago, Illinois, to pursue Dorothy's singing career. Chicago was one of the music capitals of the world at the time. Dorothy had no formal training but dreamed of singing as a professional. A friend encouraged her to try out for a female vocalist's spot in the Herbie Kay band. Kay (1904–1944) was a bandleader with a national radio show. In 1935 he would become Dorothy's first husband, although they would soon divorce in 1939. While playing on tour in Dallas, Texas, Dorothy walked through the lobby with Kay and noticed the placards announcing the orchestra would feature Dorothy *Lamour*. The *b* had been left out of her name and Kay decided he liked it, so the change was made from Lambour to Lamour. Dorothy Lamour performed on stage and radio with Kay but soon decided to try her luck in New York City, so she and her mother made the move. While in Chicago she had become acquainted with the well-known singer Rudy Vallee (1901–1986), who was a friend of Kay's. He helped introduce Lamour around town. She soon found work at several clubs, including El Morocco and The Stork Club. She was singing at a cabaret (a restaurant that provides refreshments and entertainment) when Louis B. Mayer (1885–1956), a top Hollywood studio chief, heard her and offered her a movie screen test. The catch was that she had to get herself to Hollywood, California.

Jungle princess

Lamour was appearing on the NBC radio show *Dreamer of Dreams* in 1933 when the studio decided to move the show to its Hollywood studios. Lamour made the move to Hollywood, too, and received a bit part as a chorus girl in a musical. She eventually received a contract with Paramount in 1935 but didn't appear in films again until 1936. That was the year Lamour landed the part of Ulah, a female

Tarzan type among tropical natives, in Paramount's *The Jungle Princess*. In the film, Lamour was featured in a wraparound sarong costume. She became an instant star and although she wore a sarong in only six of her fifty-nine films, it was to define her career. With her long, dark hair and trademark sarong, Lamour was a favorite pinup of thousands of U.S. servicemen during World War II.

Lamour's recordings and musical numbers in her many films helped make her one of the top box office draws in the late 1930s and the 1940s. She was best known for a series of musical-comedy films she starred in with Bob Hope (1903–2003) and Bing Crosby (1903–1977). The seven "road" movies, as they were known, were *Road to Singapore* (1940), *Road to Zanzibar* (1941), *Road to Morocco* (1942), *Road to Utopia* (1946), *Road to Rio* (1947), *Road to Bali* (1952), and *Road to Hong Kong* (1962).

Actress Dorothy Lamour volunteered so much time selling war bonds during World War II that she became known as the "the bond bombshell." *AP/Wide World Photos. Reproduced by permission.*

War bonds

When the United States declared war in December 1941, Lamour immediately contacted Henry Morgenthau, the U.S. secretary of the treasury, to volunteer her services in selling war bonds. He enthusiastically accepted her offer to sell bonds as well as to introduce a new government plan called "The War Bonds Savings Plan." Lamour would go into the war plants where aircraft, ships, and weapons were manufactured and ask the workers to invest 10 percent of their gross salaries in savings bonds. She was soon sent off in a government railroad car to collect money for the cause. Her first stop was New York City, and then she toured New England. She would travel over fifteen hundred miles through twenty-five cities in nine days. In each of these places she was greeted by thousands of people lined up on the streets. By the end of her tour, she had

Bette Davis and the Hollywood Canteen

Many members of Hollywood's entertainment community contributed to the war effort. Bette Davis (1908–1989) was among the first to volunteer her services to the U.S. State Department in order to help. She joined the "Stars Over America" program and traveled across the country to sell war bonds, raise money, and bring attention to the cause. Davis was so successful that the government requested a second tour, where she sold more bonds in one day than anyone else had in two months. At one point she sold two million dollars' worth of bonds in two days.

Davis would make a major wartime contribution when she helped establish a servicemen's club on Cahuenga Boulevard in Los Angeles, California. The Hollywood Canteen was one of the entertainment clubs set up for soldiers who were either headed to war or home on leave. Davis leased a former livery stable just one block off Sunset Boulevard and persuaded dozens of guilds and unions to donate the labor and materials to renovate and decorate the building. She enlisted the help of her agent to raise hundreds of thousands of dollars for the Canteen so that there was always a surplus of funds despite a weekly bill of three

Bette Davis points out movie servicemen serving in World War II (including Clark Gable, Ronald Reagan, and others) in the Hollywood Canteen, Los Angeles, California, 1943. *The Library of Congress.*

thousand dollars for food alone. She called on the stars to donate money and time and she served as the Canteen's president. Davis was there on opening night, October 3,

collected more than thirty million dollars in war bonds. As soon as her next film was completed, Lamour set off on her second bond tour, this time to Philadelphia, Pennsylvania. During World War II, Lamour became known as "the bond bombshell" because she dedicated so much of her time to

1942, to give the welcoming speech to over three thousand soldiers, sailors, and marines.

The Hollywood Canteen provided music, dancing, fun, and good food at no charge to the servicemen. It was a place where they could mingle with movie stars who would serve their meals, sign autographs, and pose for an endless succession of photographs. The Hollywood Canteen, with its lineup of stars, brought glamour and excitement to thousands of fighting men as the war dragged on. Increasingly the Canteen would serve wounded and disabled servicemen. Davis put together a pamphlet of instructions to help volunteers deal compassionately with these men. The sign over the entrance to the Hollywood Canteen read, "THROUGH THESE PORTALS PASS THE MOST BEAUTIFUL UNIFORMS IN THE WORLD." Davis gave long hours to ensure the Canteen's success. In the spring of 1944 she made a cameo (very brief) appearance in *Hollywood Canteen,* a Warner Brothers' film about the club. Several stars played themselves in the picture, a story about two soldiers who are given the royal treatment and a glimpse of the backstage workings in the club. The star-studded film brought in $3.3 million in profits, most of it donated to the Canteen. Upon completion of the film Davis visited Washington, D.C., where she met President Franklin D. Roosevelt.

World War II ended with the Japanese surrender in August 1945. The Hollywood Canteen closed its doors on November 22 of that year. The five hundred thousand dollars in surplus funds from its budget was applied to a veterans' relief fund. Hundreds of thousands of men had passed through the Canteen in its three years of operation. The Canteen often entertained three thousand men a night, one thousand men in each of its three shifts. In James Spada's book *More Than a Woman,* Bette Davis said, "The servicemen were all so lonesome and sad. One Christmas Eve Bing Crosby came through the kitchen door with his four little boys. He said, 'Thought maybe we could help out tonight,' and he got on that stage with those four little boys. Everything those men were fighting for were those four little boys!"

Davis received the Distinguished Civilian Service Medal, awarded by the secretary of the army to civilians who made substantial contributions to the army's mission.

selling war bonds ("bombshell" was a slang term for a very beautiful woman). While on a bond drive in 1943, Lamour met her second husband, William Ross Howard III, an Air Corps lieutenant. They would remain married for thirty-five years, until Howard's death in 1978.

Lamour's contribution to the war effort was also felt at the Hollywood Canteen (see sidebar), where she spent many hours entertaining servicemen who were on leave. One Christmas Eve she dressed as Santa Claus and played the part so effectively that no one knew she was female, let alone the famous Dorothy Lamour, until the evening was over. At the canteen, Lamour willingly took her turn serving meals to the soldiers and washing dishes when the meal was through. She could be found entertaining on the stage as well as taking a turn on the dance floor. Often servicemen just wanted to talk with her and the other celebrities they had seen so often in movies.

Live and in person

After the war ended, Lamour remained active in the entertainment world. She appeared in several films in addition to the "road" movies. She went on to tour nationally in a production of *Hello Dolly* and *Dubarry Was a Lady* in the late 1960s. In the 1980s she performed around the country in a one-woman show where she sang many of the songs from World War II and reminisced with her audience. After a long and successful career, Dorothy Lamour died in Los Angeles, California, on September 22, 1996.

For More Information

Books

Hoopes, Roy. *When the Stars Went to War: Hollywood and World War II.* New York: Random House, 1994.

Lamour, Dorothy. *My Side of the Road.* Englewood Cliffs, NJ: Prentice-Hall, 1980.

Spada, James. *More Than a Woman: An Intimate Biography of Bette Davis.* New York: Bantam Books, 1993.

Web sites

"Queen of the Road." *People Weekly.* http://www.kcmetro.cc.mo.us/pennvalley/biology/lewis/crosby/lamour.htm (accessed on July 22, 2004).

"World War Two Advertising History—War Bonds." *Ad-Access.* http://scriptorium.lib.duke.edu/adaccess/warbonds.html (accessed on July 22, 2004).

Nancy Love

Born February 14, 1914
Houghton, Michigan
Died October 22, 1976
Martha's Vineyard, Massachusetts

Aviator

Nancy Love was director of the Women's Auxiliary Ferrying Squadron, or WAFS. The WAFS was a division within the Air Transport Command of the U.S. Army. WAFS were the first women to fly for the U.S. military, serving from 1942 until 1945. By flying home front missions, Love and the WAFS were in a unique position to advance the American cause in World War II (1939–45). Her highly experienced pilots made it possible to free active-duty male pilots for combat. The WAFS were charged with transporting military aircraft between factories, modification centers, depots, and operational units.

Nancy Love was one of the most accomplished women flyers of her time. She was the first woman in U.S. military history to fly the B-25 Mitchell, the P-51 Mustang, and the Douglas C-54 Skymaster. Love was the first woman to deliver a C-47 Skytrain and one of the first two women to check out in the B-17 Flying Fortress. She was also proficient in A-36es and fourteen other types of military aircraft. Love accomplished all of this as a civil servant in the Air Transport Command because women pilots were never officially members of the U.S. military during World War II.

"Don't present us as a glamour outfit, we're not. There's no room or time for glamour in the W.A.F.S., we've got a serious job to do."

Nancy Love.
AP/Wide World Photos.
Reproduced by permission.

In 1943 several army programs were combined to form the Women's Airforce Service Pilots (WASPs). Love retained command of her original group of WAFS and continued flying military planes until Congress canceled the organization in December 1944.

Making history

Nancy Harkness was born on February 14, 1914, in Houghton, Michigan. The daughter of a wealthy physician, she attended prestigious Milton Academy in Massachusetts and Vassar College in New York. While in high school at Milton, Nancy experienced her first plane ride. Inspired, she immediately took flying lessons and within weeks received her license. At the age of sixteen, she was the youngest woman in the United States to earn a private pilot's license.

Always restless and adventurous, Nancy carried her love of flying with her to Vassar. She started a flying school and earned extra money taking students for rides in a plane she rented from a nearby airport. In 1933 she became the youngest woman to qualify for a commercial pilot's license. Nancy was an early pioneer in the development of student flying clubs in U.S. colleges and a charter member of the Ninety-Nines. The organization got its name because 99 women pilots, out of a total of 126 who were licensed at the time, joined together to form the group. The first president was well-known aviator Amelia Earhart (1897–1937).

Nancy left Vassar following her sophomore year and found a job selling airplanes on a commission basis out of the East Boston Airport in Boston, Massachusetts. In 1935 she and four other women pilots were hired by the federal government's Bureau of Air Commerce to "air-mark" the principal cities of the United States. Their job was to fly over the nation searching for landmarks such as water towers, barns, and rooftops that were visible from the air. The landmarks were then marked with city names and compass headings as aids to air navigation. It was her first regular paycheck from flying.

Love for life

Nancy Harkness met Robert Maclure Love at the East Boston Airport hangars when she first arrived in town. He was from a prominent East Coast family and had recently purchased the Curtis-Wright Air Terminal to begin his own business, Inter City Aviation. The couple married in 1936 and took off on a flying honeymoon. The union made all the Boston newspapers because women flyers were rare, and the handsome couple caught the public's interest.

After the honeymoon, Nancy returned to complete the air-marking program. In 1937 she went to work as a test pilot for the Gwinn Aircar Company in Buffalo, New York. She performed safety tests on various aircraft modifications and innovations. In one project for the Bureau of Air Commerce she tested three-wheeled landing gear, which became standard on most planes. For fun she occasionally entered the popular air races of the day. By 1938 Nancy was working full-time with her husband at Inter City Aviation. Nancy and Bob ran flying classes and charters, and they also demonstrated and sold several types of airplanes.

A changing world

When American factories began turning out warplanes for Great Britain in 1940, Nancy Love was one of several Massachusetts women who ferried light warplanes to the Canadian border. She felt it was a meaningful assignment that other experienced women pilots could do and began promoting a women's ferrying group to the army. The Loves had known many senior military officers for years through the Air Corps Reserves and Nancy was respected for her flying ability. In May 1940 she approached an old friend, Colonel Robert Olds of the Army Air Corps Planning Division, with the idea of employing women pilots to help transport planes from factories to bases. Love included a list of forty-nine women pilots she believed were well qualified. Most had flown more than a thousand hours in many kinds of aircraft. She received encouragement, but women flying airplanes and wearing pants were seen as too risqué (challenging social traditions) in America at that time.

By 1942 Love had logged more than twelve hundred flight hours. She held a Civil Aeronautics Administration (CAA) instrument card, a CAA commercial license, as well as both seaplane and high-horsepower ratings. America was

Jacqueline Cochran

When World War II (1939–45) began in 1939, the United States began a special Lend-Lease program with Great Britain. Supplies and equipment, including airplanes, were transported by way of Canada to England. In order to free male pilots for combat, the Royal Air Force (RAF) began using women pilots to fly the arriving planes to airports near their fighting units.

In July 1941 Jacqueline Cochran (1906–1980) presented General H. "Hap" Arnold, commander of the Army Air Corps, with a plan for the Army Air Corps Ferry Command to use women pilots in the United States. At the time, Arnold was of the opinion that the United States was not ready for, nor did it need, women pilots. He suggested that Cochran take a group to England for duty and by August 1942 Cochran and twenty-four other American women pilots joined the RAF Air Transport Auxiliary.

Upon her return to the United States, Cochran met with Arnold and outlined a training program to augment the Women's Auxiliary Ferrying Squadron (WAFS) in the expanding war. The new group would be called the 319th Women's Flying Training Detachment (WFTD) and would be stationed at the Municipal Airport in Houston, Texas. Jacqueline Cochran was director of this training group. She soon transferred her program to Avenger Field in Sweetwater, Texas.

More than 25,000 women applied to the program; 1,830 were accepted for training and 1,074 would eventually win their wings. They followed the Air Corps cadet program of primary, basic, and advanced flight training and ground school.

now officially involved in World War II and Robert Love, a reserve major in the Army Air Corps, received his call to active duty in Washington, D.C. Nancy Love landed a civilian post with the Air Transport Command (ATC) in Baltimore, Maryland. She commuted daily by plane from their home in Washington. The news of her employment with ATC reached Colonel William Tunner, who was head of the Ferrying Division of the ATC. At the time, new plane production was backing up at the factories and he had been searching the country for skilled pilots to ferry the planes to their final destinations. Tunner asked Love to submit a proposal for a

Jacqueline Cochran. *AP/Wide World Photos. Reproduced by permission.*

Upon graduation the pilots were sent for active duty on one of the four Ferry Command bases. They were to not only ferry planes from factories to the airfields but also test-fly repaired aircraft and even tow gunnery targets for artillery practice. They performed many other noncombat flying duties on the home front in order to release male pilots for the overseas war effort.

By July 1943 the training program was a proven success. The WFTD and the WAFS were combined so that all women pilots were under the jurisdiction of the director of women pilots, Jacqueline Cochran. They were renamed WASPs (Women's Airforce Service Pilots) and worked together until Congress canceled the organization in December 1944. They would be the last women to fly for the U.S. military for more than thirty years.

women's ferrying group that would meet the approval of General Henry H. "Hap" Arnold (1886–1950), commander of the Army Air Corps.

The WAFS

Within months, the twenty-eight-year-old Love became the director of the newly created Women's Auxiliary Ferrying Squadron, or WAFS. She soon had twenty-eight experienced female pilots under her command. Each woman had an average of eleven hundred flying hours to her credit, as well as a high-horsepower rating and a commercial flying license. Each was required to be a U.S. citizen, present two letters of recommendation, and pass the physical. The women were to remain civil servants in the Air Corps because the Ferry Division needed pilots immediately, and it would take a great deal of time to get an amendment through Congress to legally commission women pilots in the military. The WAFS were established in September 1942 and began operations at New Castle Army Airfield, Wilmington, Delaware, under ATC's 2nd Ferrying Group. The first recruits were called the Originals.

Getting the media to take the new division seriously proved difficult. *Life* magazine drew attention not to Love's flying skills, but to her beautiful legs. The War Department tried to tone down the publicity and Love herself cautioned her recruits that their personal conduct must be above reproach in order for the WAFS to succeed. Love held the allegiance of the Originals because of the opportunity she had provided them. They were not about to let her down. Hers was an elite group of pilots and Love worked hard to ensure that they flew better and faster aircraft.

On February 27, 1943, while stationed in Dallas, Texas, Love checked out in a North American P-51 Mustang, the Army Air Force's hottest fighter plane. She moved on to Long Beach, California, in order to fly some fourteen other aircraft, most of which were manufactured in the area. That same summer Love and her close friend and copilot, Betty Gillies, prepared to ferry a B-17, called the *Queen Bee,* across the Atlantic Ocean to Britain. The British had requested the delivery of one hundred of the planes for a major offensive into Europe. Colonel Tunner was faced with a big order and a lack of qualified pilots to deliver the planes. Love and Gillies had been to B-17 school and were the first women to be checked out in the Flying Fortress. They had already made three domestic deliveries to date. Tunner had been ordered to advance the WAFS to their capabilities so he cleared the two women for the delivery and assigned his personal navigator to the flight. The crew picked up the *Queen Bee* in Cincinnati, Ohio, and flew it to Goose Bay, Labrador, in Canada. While awaiting clearance to fly the final leg of their journey to Prestwick, Scotland, an

urgent message arrived from General Arnold, who was away visiting in London, England. It said, "Cease and desist, no WAFS will fly outside the contiguous U.S." Bitterly disappointed that they had been grounded by politics, the two women shut down the engines.

Four members of the United States Women's Airforce Service Pilots (WASPs) receiving instructions as they chart a cross-country course. *National Archives.*

Grounded

The WAFS were merged with the army's WFTD (Women's Flying Training Detachment) in 1943. The combination was called WASPs (Women's Airforce Service Pilots). Nancy Love remained in charge of all ferrying operations and so her Originals in the WAFS remained secure in their existing assignments.

December 1944 saw the end of the Women's Airforce Service Pilots and the women were grounded. Love stayed on duty for a short time to assist with writing the Air Transport

Command's Report. She finished her wartime service with another women's aviation first when she went on a flight around the world. She was at the controls of the plane at least one-half of the time, including the leg of the journey crossing over the Himalayas.

In July 1946 Nancy and Bob Love became the first couple in history to be decorated at the same time for their military service. Nancy was presented with the Air Medal for her pioneering work with the Ferry Division while Bob added a Distinguished Service Medal to his other decorations. In 1948, shortly after the U.S. Air Force was established, Nancy Love was designated a lieutenant colonel in the U.S. Air Force Reserves.

After the war, the Loves withdrew to private life and started a family. They had three daughters and moved to Martha's Vineyard, Massachusetts. Nancy Love kept the women she had commanded central in her life until her death from cancer on October 22, 1976. Love never stopped working to gain formal recognition as military veterans for women who served as pilots in World War II. They received this status in 1977, shortly after her death.

For More Information

Books

Carl, Ann B. *A Wasp Among Eagles*. Washington, DC: Smithsonian Institution Press, 1999.

Granger, Byrd Howell. *On Final Approach*. Scottsdale, AZ: Falconer Publishing, 1991.

Knapp, Sally. *New Wings For Women*. New York: Thomas Y. Crowell Company, 1946.

Verges, Marianne. *On Silver Wings*. New York: Random House, 1991.

Williams, Vera S. *WASPS—Women Airforce Service Pilots of World War II*. Osceola, WI: Motorbooks International, 1994.

Web sites

"Fly Girls: Nancy Harkness Love." *PBS: The American Experience.* http://www.pbs.org/wgbh/amex/flygirls/peopleevents/pandeAMEX03.html (accessed on July 22, 2004).

"Jacqueline Cochran, Record Setter." *National Aviation Hall of Fame.* http://www.nationalaviation.org/website/index.asp?webpageid={F3401AC2-408C-42A7-AD0F-CDDC7942F110}&eID=244 (accessed on July 22, 2004).

"Nancy Harkness Love." *Airlift/Tanker Association—Hall of Fame.* http://www.atalink.org/hallfame/harkness.html (accessed on July 22, 2004).

Bill Mauldin

Born October 29, 1921
Mountain Park, New Mexico
Died January 22, 2003
Newport Beach, California

Cartoonist

Bill Mauldin was one of the twentieth century's outstanding editorial cartoonists. The Pulitzer Prize-winning artist portrayed World War II's (1939–45) grim reality, laced with his own brand of humor, and in so doing he immortalized the American serviceman. He was considered a great reporter and was also credited with being a positive influence on morale for the armed services during the war.

Mauldin's cartoon characters, Willie and Joe, slogged their way through battle-scarred Europe surviving the enemy and the elements with their humor intact. They mirrored the lives of soldiers in the European theater as they encountered the blunders and efficiency, the irritations and comradeship, of life in the army.

Mauldin interpreted World War II for the soldiers, also called GIs, as well as for Americans at home. His popular cartoons were reprinted and widely circulated in U.S. newspapers. This exposure allowed him to tell the story of the lives of soldiers to people on the home front and made America smile when it needed to most.

Growing up in the West

William Henry Mauldin was born on October 29, 1921, on the family farm at Mountain Park, near Santa Fe in New Mexico. Katrina Bemis and Sidney Mauldin proudly named their second son after his paternal grandfather, William Henry Mauldin. Bill and his brother, Sidney Junior (Sid), lived on the mountain apple farm with their parents and had their maternal grandparents close by. They enjoyed a happy childhood, but money was always tight. Sidney Mauldin decided to try other ventures and moved his family to a variety of western locations. From mining in Parral, Chihuahua, Mexico, to homesteading in the desert west of Phoenix, Arizona, the outcome was always the same and the family would return home to Mountain Park. When the Mauldins' marriage ended in divorce, Bill and Sid moved back to Phoenix together to finish their high school education.

Cartooning

Bill enjoyed drawing pictures from an early age. While thumbing through a copy of *Popular Mechanics* magazine at the age of thirteen, he came across a group of ads for cartoonists' correspondence schools. Bill selected the Landon School in Cleveland, Ohio, because its advertisement noted that some practitioners of this art made as much as a hundred thousand dollars a year. It was the fourth year of the Great Depression (1929–41) and Bill thought he had found the answer to all his problems. The Great Depression was a severe economic crisis starting in the United States in late 1929 that soon spread throughout the world during the 1930s.

While attending Phoenix Union High School, Bill solved his clothing budget problem by joining the ROTC battalion, which required members to wear uniforms four days each week. Several teachers at the school took an interest in Bill because of his artistic talent and directed him to the Chicago Academy of Fine Arts, in Chicago, Illinois, which had a good cartooning department.

Military service

Bill Mauldin finished his year at the Chicago Academy in 1940 and enlisted in the Arizona National Guard, which was

Pvt. Robert L. Bowman, left, poses for artist Sgt. Bill Mauldin in Anzio, Italy, in May 1944, during World War II. The finished sketch would become known as "G.I. Joe." *AP/Wide World Photos. Reproduced by permission.*

part of the 45th Infantry Division. The 45th was about to become the very first Guard division to be federalized, or made a part of the regular army. Mauldin was initially assigned as a rifleman, but once his cartooning abilities were discovered he was attached to headquarters staff at *Division News*, the newspaper for the 45th Division. It was here that he honed his craft and began to develop his most famous characters, Willie and Joe, two riflemen in World War II. When Mauldin's division shipped overseas, the army daily newspaper, *Stars and Stripes*, began publishing his drawings as well.

Mauldin's characters were usually infantrymen, sometimes combat medics, and occasionally artillerymen. However, they were always haggard and full of the line soldier's practical point of view. They were also men who always got the job done. Mauldin was convinced that the infantry was the group in the army that gave more and got less than anybody else did. Mauldin never fought as a line soldier but spent much of his time with line companies in Italy, one of the grimmest theaters

This cartoon is one example of Bill Mauldin's famous depictions of "Willie and Joe," characters Mauldin created while serving as a U.S. Army rifleman during World War II. The cartoons lifted the spirits of the soldiers while showing Americans back home the realities of the soldier's life—with some humor added. *AP/Wide World Photos. Reproduced by permission.*

"Me future is settled, Willie. I'm gonna be a perfessor on types o' European soil."

of the war. His visits to the front were reflected in the reality of his cartoons. As an enlisted man, he gave the soldiers hope and an occasional laugh on the battlefield. He drew pictures of the infantry because he understood what their perilous life was like.

Willie and Joe began as clean-shaven recruits and progressed to unshaven, bone-weary infantrymen. The characters

James Montgomery Flagg

While Norman Rockwell (1894–1978) painted rural America, James Montgomery Flagg (1877–1960) focused on the urban ideals. Born in 1877, Flagg was a child prodigy (child having extraordinary talent) whose talent saw him earning a steady income as an artist in all the popular magazines of the day by the time he was a teenager. Flagg was outspoken and lived a decidedly bohemian (not living by conventional values) lifestyle. His healthy ego served him well in the highly competitive illustration markets of the day.

Flagg's work featured many of his favorite models. His wife, Nellie, appeared in numerous illustrations, but the majority of his models were professional. They became known as "Flagg girls," and they were highlighted in books and posters, as well as every major magazine published at the time. These women always reflected the artist's view of the ideal woman rather than any current fad regarding beauty. His definition of that ideal, centered around classic

Flagg's famous painting featuring Uncle Sam.
AP/Wide World Photos. Reproduced by permission.

femininity and graceful poise, never changed throughout the years of his career.

were soldiers who had been in the war for several years, and they portrayed the tedium and treachery of war to the American people. The two characters were all but indistinguishable from one another by design. If anything set them apart it was Joe's hook-nose compared to Willie's rounded one.

Mauldin's cartoons drew many laughs but also some high-ranking criticism from those who felt officers were not portrayed in the most favorable light. Mauldin's nonconformist

Flagg was also a contributor to the new medium of silent films, both as an actor and as a writer. The films were so well received that during World War I (1914–18) he was asked to write promotional films for the marines and the American Red Cross. During this time, Flagg recorded the movement of America in his countless illustrations that appeared in every prominent magazine in the country. He was already too old to fight by the time World War I erupted and so New York governor Charles S. Whitman (1868–1947) appointed Flagg as State Military Artist in 1917.

Although he produced forty-five other posters for the government, Flagg's most famous painting was of Uncle Sam pointing at the viewer with the caption "I Want YOU for the U.S. Army" (1917). Flagg himself was the model for the character of Uncle Sam. President Franklin D. Roosevelt (1882–1945; served 1933–45) wrote to praise him for his resourcefulness in saving the cost of a model. The truth was that Flagg had an ideal prototype of masculine good looks and charm, just as he did for females, and he felt that he represented the male ideal as well as any of his models.

Flagg chose to transform the formerly benign old man of the "stars and stripes" into a compelling leader who meant business. His original watercolor drawing of Uncle Sam appeared on the cover of *Leslie's Weekly* magazine before it was considered for the military poster. The poster was to become the most famous of both World Wars and was to appear in several variations. The changes reflected the temper of the times both in mood and tastes. Originally drawn in decorative pen and ink washes in the first war, the posters for World War II (1939–45) were splashy and contrived by comparison. An estimated four million copies of the poster were issued in World War I, with another four hundred thousand printed for World War II.

approach brought him a face-to-face chastising from General George Patton (1885–1945), who felt that any characters representing the U.S. military should be neat and clean-shaven. For his part, Mauldin disliked Patton's insistence on battlefield "spit and polish" and for what he felt was Patton's low regard for the GIs. However, many officers enjoyed the cartoons and felt Mauldin's humor was good for troop morale, so he continued drawing without censorship. His art allowed soldiers to laugh at themselves as well as their leaders, and still move forward in their purpose.

Recognition

In 1945, at age twenty-three, his series *Up Front With Mauldin* won Mauldin the first of his two Pulitzer Prizes for editorial cartooning. He also appeared on the cover of *Time* magazine and had the country's number one best-selling book in *Up Front*.

After the war, Mauldin went on to draw cartoons about the soldier's difficult transition back to civilian life on the home front. Any recognition or honor Mauldin received personally was used to direct attention back to the plight of the returning soldier in America. He worked to create a sense of appreciation for the endless sacrifice of those coming home from the war. He wanted to ensure they would be taken back into civilian life and given a chance to be themselves again when the war was over.

Mauldin freelanced for a time, and then in 1958 he joined the St. Louis *Post-Dispatch* as an editorial cartoonist. It was there that he won a second Pulitzer Prize in 1959. In 1962 Mauldin moved to the Chicago *Sun-Times,* where he was to draw one of his most poignant and famous cartoons on the day of President John F. Kennedy's (1917–1963; served 1961–63) assassination. The drawing showed a grieving President Abraham Lincoln (1809–1865; served 1861–65), his hands covering his face, at the Lincoln Memorial.

Career highlights

Mauldin wrote and illustrated sixteen books during his lifetime. He also acted in two movies, including John Huston's (1906–1987) 1951 production of *The Red Badge of Courage,* starring real-life war hero Audie Murphy (1924–1971). Mauldin continued his life's work as a political cartoonist until his retirement in 1992. He moved back to Santa Fe, New Mexico, and began to sculpt much of his early cartoon work. Mauldin had seven sons from his three marriages. They cared for him until he died of complications from Alzheimer's disease at the age of eighty-one in a nursing home in Newport Beach, California, on January 22, 2003.

For More Information

Books

Mauldin, Bill. *The Brass Ring.* New York: W.W. Norton, 1971.

Mauldin, Bill. *A Sort of a Saga.* New York: William Sloane Associates Publishers, 1949.

Mauldin, Bill. *Up Front.* Cleveland and New York: World Publishing, 1945.

Meyer, Susan E. *James Montgomery Flagg.* New York: Watson-Guptill Publishers, 1974.

Web sites

"In Memorium: Bill Mauldin." *PBS Online News Hour.* http://www.pbs.org/newshour/bb/remember/jan-june03/mauldin_12-23.html (accessed on July 22, 2004).

"James Montgomery Flagg." *Spartacus Educational.* http://www.spartacus.schoolnet.co.uk/artflagg.htm (accessed on July 22, 2004).

"William Henry 'Bill' Mauldin, Sergeant, United States Army." *Arlington National Cemetery Website.* http://www.arlingtoncemetery.net/whmauldin.htm (accessed on July 22, 2004).

Luisa Moreno

Born August 30, 1907
Guatemala City, Guatemala
Died November 4, 1992
Guatemala

Labor leader

Luisa Moreno was a trade union leader and a civil rights activist. Fluent in both English and Spanish, she was a major figure in the struggle for Hispanic civil rights and fair treatment for nearly three decades. During World War II (1939–45), Moreno's efforts led to better pay and working conditions for women workers, particularly Hispanic workers in the war industries.

While the U.S. economy was booming in the mid-1920s, many workers emigrated from Mexico to the United States. However, when the Great Depression (1929–41), a period of high unemployment and decreased business activity through the 1930s, began, the U.S. government enforced the Mexican Repatriation Program. This program forced hundreds of thousands of Mexican Americans back into Mexico until the United States once again needed them for the work force during World War II. With the repatriation program in force after 1929, the pace of Mexican American labor organizing accelerated in order to protect the civil rights of the Hispanic community.

Moreno was the first Hispanic vice president of a major U.S. trade union and became state vice president for the

Congress of Industrial Organizations (CIO), a major national labor organization. As a founding member of the Spanish-Speaking Peoples' Congress, Moreno started the first national effort to bring Hispanic workers together from diverse ethnic backgrounds. She was active in the fight to end racial tension in Southern California and worked to end violent outbreaks between whites and Hispanics in 1943.

Coming to America

Born in 1907 in Guatemala, Luisa Moreno came of age in the United States. In Guatemala her family was considered upper middle class. Her parents sent her to an elite parochial school, the College of the Holy Names, in Oakland, California, for her education. As a teenager, she organized a group of her peers to successfully lobby for the admission of women into Guatemalan universities. Moreno decided against attending university herself and instead moved to Mexico, where she worked as a journalist. In 1928 she followed her Mexican artist husband to the art world of New York City, where she gave birth to her only daughter, Mytyl. The couple separated three years later and Moreno went to work as a seamstress in a Spanish Harlem sweatshop. The miserable conditions there led her to become one of America's first Hispanic labor organizers.

Moreno eventually moved to California and made San Diego her home base. She became an international representative of the United Cannery, Agricultural, Packing and Allied Workers of America (UCAPAWA), the first CIO local with a Mexican female majority membership. She traveled the nation visiting neighborhoods and speaking to local *mutualistas* or mutual aid societies. These societies were social and cultural support groups for the Hispanic American population.

During her career, Moreno organized a wide variety of unions ranging from cigar factory workers in New York, Pennsylvania, and Florida, to pecan processing workers in San Antonio, Texas. UCAPAWA staged a successful strike against the California Sanitary Canning Company in 1939. The strike proved to be an important event in the annals of Mexican American labor history as it won the union recognition and a smaller decrease in wages than had been expected. Moreno, as the union vice president, led organizing efforts over the next two years expanding membership throughout Southern California.

In 1938 Moreno helped found El Congreso de Pueblos de Habla Hispana (The Spanish-Speaking Peoples' Congress). The first conference, held in Los Angeles, California, in 1939, called for an end to segregation in public facilities, housing, education, and employment. More than a labor union, the organization was a civil rights assembly dedicated to winning equal rights for all Hispanic Americans. Pragmatic, tough-minded, and a charismatic leader, Moreno was convinced that uniting together and seeking political compromise would reap the most benefit for the common, poorly educated worker.

Becoming American

President **Franklin D. Roosevelt** (1882–1945; served 1933–45; see entry) instituted many measures to combat the ills of the Great Depression, and he was seen as a champion for the poor. Roosevelt was admired by Hispanic Americans for his compassion as well as for his government's Good Neighbor Policy. The policy, named in 1934, made it clear that the United States would no longer intervene militarily in Latin American affairs. The good relations it engendered would pay off during World War II, when the United States enjoyed the close cooperation of Mexico and other Latin American countries on the Allied side.

The United States did not immediately enter World War II but mobilized industry on the home front to improve its own defenses and to supply countries fighting the Axis powers of Germany, Japan, and Italy. This mobilization that stepped up dramatically once the United States entered the war in December 1941 pulled the country out of the Great Depression. Suddenly jobs in defense and other industries were widely available, even more so as conscription and voluntary enlistment put more than sixteen million Americans in uniform.

While Moreno was organizing union workers in Southern California, World War II was transforming the region into a giant military base and factory. By July 1942 the United States had been at war for eight months and was facing an indefinite period in which much of its working population

Hispanic Americans and World War II

Hispanic Americans participated fully in all combat campaigns of World War II (1939–45), both in the European and Pacific theaters. They fought side by side with non-Hispanic Americans for a common cause and a shared national purpose. Unlike black Americans, they experienced little discrimination in the armed forces. After the war they benefited from the GI Bill, which financed higher education and offered low-cost loans to buy homes and establish businesses.

Despite the sacrifices Hispanic Americans made in the defense of their country in World War II, the struggle for full acceptance as Americans in civilian life was far from over. However, the experience of war had changed their collective focus. Having lost comrades and risked their own lives to defend their country, Hispanic Americans became more conscious of the world outside their own communities. They were more determined to demand the constitutional rights due to them as Americans.

Luisa Moreno's political activity helped a generation of Hispanic Americans, who came of age in World War II, to share in expanding federal policies banning racial discrimination and increasing protection of civil rights through the following decades.

would be overseas. Temporary laborers were needed to fill their places at home.

The U.S. and Mexican governments worked together to set up the Bracero Program, which brought hundreds of thousands of Mexicans into the country during the war. Their labor in agriculture made it possible to fill wartime demands for food. The Mexican term *bracero* comes from the Spanish word *brazo* or "arm." Roughly translated, *bracero* means "hired hand" in English. Mexico was still stinging with memories of the recent repatriation act. It agreed, as a friend and ally, to supply braceros to the United States but asked for safeguards to avoid their exploitation. Because of Mexico's severe unemployment and low wages, more than two hundred thousand Mexicans participated in the program by the time the war ended. Although contracts were signed, in practice they were routinely violated and the workers were subjected to a variety of abuses.

Zoot suits and pachucos

The introduction of large numbers of immigrants triggered anxiety and renewed long-held prejudices in increasingly crowded California. As a labor consultant, Luisa Moreno found herself defending the new immigrants against the conservative anti-Mexican movement. As wartime stress mounted, Moreno was also called upon to participate in the Sleepy Lagoon case in Los Angeles.

On August 2, 1942, a young Mexican American named Jose Diaz was found dead near the Sleepy Lagoon swimming hole. A gang fight had been reported near the scene the day before, and twenty-two Hispanic youth gang members involved in that fight were tried for the crime. The media frenzy that followed focused on the *pachuco* gangs in Los Angeles. Pachuco is a type of slang that became associated with Hispanic youths, and the word itself came to mean "tough guy." In the early 1940s the pachucos had adopted an outfit known as the zoot suit. The suit consisted of a long coat worn with a high-waist, tight-cuffed pant, and the outfit was usually topped with a broad-brimmed hat. A long, ducktail haircut and hanging watch chain completed the look. White Americans associated the zoot suit with gangs and crime.

Despite a lack of evidence and numerous violations of their civil rights, twelve of the defendants in the Sleepy Lagoon case were found guilty of murder in January 1943. In reaction, Luisa Moreno and other supporters formed the Sleepy Lagoon Defense Committee. Through their efforts, in October 1944, an appeals court reversed the convictions and dismissed all charges. However, the high-profile trial coverage had already caused widespread damage in promoting anti-Mexican sentiment.

The zoot suit riots

Coming in a time of war when many young Americans were enlisted in the military, the Sleepy Lagoon case called attention to the perceived character of those on trial. In June 1943 the tension erupted into full-scale violence in Los Angeles.

Minor skirmishes between white servicemen on furlough (approved leave of absence) and pachucos in zoot suits began as a series of street brawls before escalating into a full-fledged race riot. The riots, fueled by sensationalist media, quickly spread to Pasadena, Long Beach, and San Diego. Working to end the violence, Luisa Moreno attempted to mediate the conflicts between San Diego's Mexican American community and the U.S. military. At the same time, she continued her work supporting community organizations such as Mothers of the Hispanic Soldier.

Deported

Moreno's World War II organizing efforts jeopardized her own residency in the United States. Over the years, Moreno's political life had brought her into conflict with state senator Jack B. Tenney of Los Angeles. When Moreno retired and married navy veteran Gray Dayton Bemis, she petitioned the Immigration and Naturalization Service (INS) for American citizenship. A sense of fear was sweeping the country at that time. Even the accusation of membership in the Communist party was enough to ruin a person's reputation. Passports could be taken away and jobs and promotions denied. The government closely monitored those under suspicion. Many political leaders in the labor movement were charged with being Communists because of their unpopular union work. Moreno came under investigation by the California State Committee on Un-American Activities led by Tenney. She was offered citizenship in exchange for testifying at the deportation hearing of other labor leaders. Moreno refused, and Tenney had her deported as a dangerous alien on November 30, 1950.

Luisa Moreno and Gray Bemis left the United States, never to return again. They initially went to Chihuahua, Mexico, but later lived in several other Latin American countries as well. Moreno eventually moved back to her native Guatemala, only to flee in 1954 when the U.S.-backed coup of the Guatemalan government threw the nation into chaos. In her final years Moreno returned to Guatemala, where, isolated and incapacitated by old age, she died on November 4, 1992. Her will stipulated that she wanted to be cremated, but her brother, Ernesto, opposed it, and she was buried in the family's marble mausoleum instead.

For More Information

Books

Gonzalez, Juan. *Harvest of Empire: A History of Latinos in America.* New York: Viking, 2000.

Kanellos, Nicolas. *Hispanic Firsts: 500 Years of Extraordinary Achievement.* Detroit, MI: Gale Research, 1997.

May, Elaine Tyler. "Pushing the Limits: 1940–1961." In *No Small Courage: A History of Women in the United States,* edited by Nancy F. Cott. New York: Oxford University Press, 2000.

Meier, Matt S., and Feliciano Ribera. *Mexican Americans, American Mexicans: From Conquistadors to Chicanos.* New York: Hill and Wang, 1972.

Ochoa, George. *Atlas of Hispanic-American History.* New York: Media Projects, 2001.

Shorris, Earl. *Latinos: A Biography of the People.* New York: W.W. Norton, 1992.

Takaki, Ronald. *A Different Mirror: A History of Multicultural America.* Boston: Little, Brown and Company, 1993.

Web sites

"Becoming American: A Cautionary Tale." *University of Southern Florida, Latin American & Caribbean Studies.* http://w3.usf.edu/~lacs/editorials-mckiernan-gonzalez.html (accessed on July 22, 2004).

"Luisa Moreno and the Beginnings of the Mexican American Civil Rights Movement in San Diego." *The Journal of San Diego History.* http://www.sandiegohistory.org/journal/97summer/moreno.htm (accessed on July 22, 2004).

Mine Okubo

Born June 27, 1912
Riverside, California
Died February 10, 2001
New York, New York

Artist

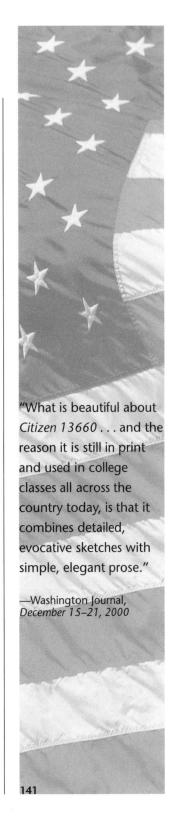

Born an American citizen, Mine Okubo had never been to Japan and spoke little Japanese. Yet she was imprisoned during World War II (1939–45) along with 112,000 other Japanese Americans because of her Japanese ancestry. Before the war, Mine was building an art career through academic studies in California and training in Europe. She would later apply her artistic skills to record her almost two years in the stark, isolated internment camps. The resulting drawings and written accounts would document this gross injustice toward a segment of the American population for later generations to learn from. She also managed to establish a highly acclaimed, longstanding art career following her imprisonment.

An artist mother

The daughter of Japanese parents, Mine Okubo was born on June 27, 1912, in Riverside, California. She had several brothers and sisters. Her mother had graduated from the Tokyo Art Institute and was a painter. In 1903 Japan had sent her to the St. Louis Exposition of Arts and Crafts to show her work.

Mine was greatly influenced by her mother. Her father was a landscaper and gardener. They were poor but made do.

Mine Okubo attended Riverside Junior College in 1933 and 1934, where she was an art student. From there she went to the University of California at Berkeley. While going to school she worked at various jobs such as a seamstress, housemaid, agricultural fieldworker, waitress, and tutor. At Berkeley, Okubo learned the art techniques of fresco and mural painting. She earned her bachelor's degree in 1935 and a master's degree in fine arts in 1936. In 1938 Okubo won Berkeley's highest art honor, the Bertha Taussig Traveling Scholarship. Okubo had an artist uncle who spent much time in Paris, France, and she was eager to learn from the art tradition there. Although her uncle died before she began her trip, Okubo continued with the trip as planned, traveling widely in Europe for eighteen months while living on a very modest budget. In Paris she studied under noted painter Fernand Leger (1881–1955). She also experienced art elsewhere, including England, Sicily, and Italy. The trip greatly influenced Okubo's art style.

World War II begins in Europe

In September 1939, when Germany invaded Poland, Okubo was traveling in Switzerland. Because of newly introduced travel restrictions due to the war, it took three months to return to her place in France. She then received word her mother was seriously ill. Okubo decided it was time to end her journey and return to the United States. Her mother died shortly after her return. Okubo moved back to Berkeley, taking her younger brother, Toku, who enrolled in college at Berkeley. She found work in the New Deal's Federal Arts Project. She demonstrated fresco painting at the Golden Gate International Exposition and worked with famous Mexican artist Diego Rivera (1886–1957). (The New Deal referred to a collection of government programs created to bring relief and recovery to citizens suffering under the worst U.S. economic crisis in history, the Great Depression [1929–41].) Rivera greatly influenced her with the social themes in his art. Like many other artists during the Depression, Okubo's work became influenced by the human and social problems she saw around her.

Enemy aliens

Following the surprise Japanese bombing of Pearl Harbor in Hawaii on December 7, 1941, Japanese Americans were labeled enemy aliens along with German and Italian Americans. Within weeks of the attack, President **Franklin D. Roosevelt** (1882–1945; served 1933–45; see entry) ordered the removal of 112,000 Japanese Americans from the West Coast. A great hysteria among the public had grown about potential Japanese attacks on the mainland. Japanese Americans were suspected of being potential spies and saboteurs despite any evidence to support those notions.

Okubo's father, because of his active participation in traditional Japanese religious organizations, was considered a particular threat, perhaps even working for the Japanese government. The U.S. government sent him to a detention camp in Missoula, Montana, and later to Louisiana. At the time of evacuation, Okubo was doing mosaics for the Oakland Hospitality House.

As ordered by the government, on April 26, 1942, Japanese and Japanese Americans on the West Coast were to report to various relocation stations. Okubo reported to a central relocation station established at Berkeley's First Congregational Church. She and her brother were assigned a number that would be their personal identification for the next few years: 13660. They were given three days to settle their affairs and report for relocation. On May 1 she and Toku were taken to the Tanforan Race Track in San Bruno, California, where they stayed for six months. Families were forced to live in the only available housing at Tanforan: old horse stalls. Her brother had been scheduled to receive his bachelor's degree from the University of California at Berkeley only a few weeks later. Like Mine and Toku, two-thirds of the 112,000 Japanese Americans relocated were American citizens. When the permanent relocation camps were finished being constructed away from the Coast, they were sent to the Topaz camp in the high desert country of Utah for the next one and a half years.

The family was widely scattered. Besides her father being taken to Montana and Louisiana, Okubo's older sister was sent to Heart Mountain in Wyoming. An older brother was drafted into the U.S. military from Riverside. The military did not realize at the time that he was a Japanese American.

Japanese evacuees during World War II are pictured at the Tanforan Assembly Center in California preparing to depart for a permanent relocation center in Utah on September 15, 1942.
© Corbis. Reproduced by permission.

Sketching camp experiences

Life in the relocation camp was always a challenge. For example, when camp authorities discovered Okubo and her brother were siblings and not husband and wife, they tried to separate them but she successfully resisted. In camp Okubo began sketching scenes of daily life. Cameras and photographs were not permitted in the camps. She quit drawing in the bright energetic colors she had learned to use in Europe and at Berkeley and turned to more stark black-and-white drawings, reflecting the moods of imprisonment. At Tanforan she completed as many as fifty drawings in a single month. In all, she made some two thousand drawings. To keep from being interrupted while drawing, Okubo would nail a quarantine sign on her door.

Okubo wanted to capture the pain of confinement in her artwork. Her work also vividly portrayed Japanese American culture at the time. The collection would be published by

Columbia University Press in 1946 titled *Citizen 13660*. It was the first published account of Japanese internment.

In the Topaz camp, Okubo joined with others who had college publication experience to start a camp literary magazine called *Trek*. In three issues, published in December 1942 and February and June 1943, the publication relayed camp experiences. Okubo contributed the cover illustrations, which depicted various experiences of the camp detainees. The first cover showed a family in camp preparing for Christmas.

Developing a normal family life was difficult in the camps. Parents were trying to raise children while encircled by barbed wire. The detainees had to build a complex community in the desert, including homes, schools, churches, and even a jail, from scratch with few materials available. The parents who had worked so hard to give their children opportunities in America had lost it all in a short period of time. Okubo's art showed how painful it was for the detainees to be shoved aside by American society. Okubo was imprisoned for almost two years, from May 1942 to January 1944, before being released with proof of having gained outside employment. Many other Japanese Americans spent more than three years before being released.

Work in New York

Okubo mailed one of her camp sketches to an art show in San Francisco, California. It won an award and led to a job with *Fortune* magazine to illustrate articles. In January 1944 she moved to New York and began working on the April *Fortune* issue that focused on Japan. However, being Japanese American, Okubo still faced discrimination and had a hard time renting an apartment in New York.

Okubo's art quickly gained attention. Besides doing illustrations, she resumed her painting. In 1944 she held an art exhibit at the Rockefeller Center in New York. In 1945 she participated in a traveling art show that included paintings and drawings of Japanese relocation camps. The Riverside Public Library, located in her hometown, showed her work in 1946.

Okubo continued to work as an independent (freelance) illustrator for the next ten years. Her work was published

Japanese American Relocation Camps

Some 127,000 people of Japanese descent lived in the United States at the time of the Japanese attack on Pearl Harbor, Hawaii, on December 7, 1941. Most of them, some 112,000, lived on the West Coast. Two-thirds were native–born U.S. citizens and the remainder were immigrants who held no U.S. citizenship because of existing immigration laws preventing Asian immigrants from acquiring citizenship.

Following Pearl Harbor, public fears of Japanese espionage and sabotage dramatically rose. On February 19, 1942, President Franklin D. Roosevelt (1882–1945; served 1933–45) signed the Japanese American removal order, Executive Order 9066, with the War Relocation Authority (WRA) in charge. Japanese Americans had to register at WRA control stations by the end of March, where each family was issued a number and assigned a time to report for removal. Since they could only bring what they could carry, they had to hastily sell their businesses and possessions. The evacuees were first taken to temporary holding areas called assembly centers, usually located at fairgrounds, exposition centers, stockyards, and racetracks, where they would stay for several months.

The WRA built ten permanent relocation camps in seven states, mostly located in the remote, barren desert country of California (2), Arizona (2), Utah, Wyoming, Colorado, and Idaho. Two other camps

in most leading magazines including *Fortune, Life,* and *Time,* newspapers like the *New York Times,* and children's and medical books. She continued to focus her own artwork on social issues in the United States. After her war internment experience, Okubo turned more to Japanese folk art for inspiration, steering away from her American roots.

A celebrated artist

From 1950 to 1952 Okubo returned to Berkeley to lecture in art. She appeared in a 1965 CBS television news program on Japanese American internment. During this time she presented various art exhibits from California to Massachusetts, winning many awards for her work. Her work also appeared in were placed in Arkansas. The camps were surrounded with barbed wire and armed guards and consisted of wooden barracks and community bathing, toilet, and eating facilities. Privacy was nonexistent and sanitation poor. Thin walls divided the barracks into small one-room apartments lit with bare light bulbs. Cots were provided for sleeping. A family shared each apartment.

By 1943 those who found employment were allowed to leave, and some thirty-five thousand were able to do so. The government released all remaining detainees in December 1944. The detention of Japanese Americans was one of the great tragedies on the American home front during World War II (1939–45). In addition to being denied their legal rights to challenge their imprisonment, the detainees lost an estimated four hundred million dollars in property and income. No Japanese American was ever charged with war crimes. In fact, some thirty-three thousand Japanese Americans served in the U.S. armed forces during World War II, fighting for the very government that imprisoned their families on the home front. A Japanese American regiment fighting in Europe became the most decorated army unit of World War II. More than four decades after the internment of Japanese Americans in the United States, a formal U.S. government apology was issued in 1988 by President Ronald Reagan (1911–2004; served 1981–1989).

various publications, including a 1970 *Time-Life* book on life in the 1940s and 1950s. In 1972 she had her first major show on the West Coast, held at the Oakland Museum. Her book, *Citizen 13660* (1983), won the 1984 American Book Award. The book was still used in classrooms in the early twenty-first century. In 1991 Okubo received a Lifetime Achievement Award from the Women's Caucus for Art.

Okubo never married, seeking instead the independence of an individual dedicated to her art and a search for her own self-identity, and a lifelong student of the human condition. Her art can be found in various museums and shows across the United States. She died on February 10, 2001, at her home in the Greenwich Village section of New York City. She left the works she exhibited at the 1972 Oakland show to the Oakland Museum.

For More Information

Books

Okubo, Mine. *Citizen 13660.* Columbia University Press, 1983.

Stanley, Jerry. *I Am an American: The True Story of Japanese Internment.* New York: Crown, 1994.

Sun, Shirley. *Mine Okubo: An American Experience.* San Francisco: East Wind Printers, 1972.

Takaki, Ronald T. *Democracy and Race: Asian Americans and World War II.* New York: Chelsea House, 1995.

Periodicals

Nash, Phil. "Mine Okubo: Celebrating Art." *Washington Journal* (December 15–21, 2000). Available at http://www.asianweek.com/ 2000_12_15/news7_washj.html.

Web sites

Japanese American National Museum. http://www.janm.org (accessed on July 24, 2004).

National Japanese American Historical Society. http://www.nikkeiheritage. org (accessed on July 24, 2004).

A. Philip Randolph

Born April 15, 1889
Crescent City, Florida
Died May 16, 1979
New York, New York

Labor and civil rights leader

"Why should a Negro worker be penalized for being black?"

During World War II (1939–45), A. Philip Randolph fought racial discrimination in war industries and the armed services. His efforts built a foundation for the civil rights movement of the 1950s and 1960s. A. Philip Randolph was one of the most influential black American leaders of the twentieth century.

Early life

A. Philip Randolph was born on April 15, 1889, the second of two sons born to a poor family in Crescent City, Florida. His father, an itinerant minister who traveled about the area to various small rural churches, also worked as a tailor to provide for his family. The Randolph family emphasized religion and education. In 1903 Randolph attended Cookman Institute, an all-black male Methodist school, where he excelled. In addition to being a good athlete, he showed particular skill at drama, public speaking, singing, and literature. Randolph graduated in 1907 at the top of his class. Following graduation, Randolph worked at odd jobs in Jacksonville,

A. Philip Randolph.
The Library of Congress.

Florida, while giving public readings, singing, and acting in plays. In search of better job opportunities and less racial discrimination in the North, in April 1911 Randolph joined the great migration of Southern blacks moving to the North. Randolph headed to Harlem in New York City, where he held various jobs including waiter, porter, and elevator operator. He also joined a theater club where he tackled Shakespearean plays. Through these parts, Randolph developed public speaking skills that would benefit him through much of his life. Randolph married a fellow theater club member in November 1914. They would have no children.

Seeking to establish a more stable career, Randolph abandoned acting and enrolled in City College of New York. The college offered a free education for those with strong academic skills. At college, Randolph became interested in politics and organized his own political group, the Independent Political Council.

Political activism

In New York, Randolph met Chandler Owen (1889–1967), a student at Columbia Law School. They were attracted to the growing labor union activity in the United States that was seeking improved working conditions, such as a forty-hour workweek. Union activity was considered a radical movement in the 1910s. They also joined the Socialist Party in late 1916. The party promoted the rights of individual citizens over dominance of big business. Randolph and Owen often stood on street corners in Harlem promoting the ideas of socialism and calling for blacks to join unions. Yet to most blacks, socialism and unions represented a white man's world with little relevance to them.

In 1917 Randolph organized a union of elevator operators. He and Owen were also hired to publish *Hotel Messenger,* a newsletter for the Headwaiters and Sidewaiters Society of Greater New York. However, their positions on labor issues were too radical for the organization, and after only eight months, Randolph and Owen were fired. They created their own magazine simply called the *Messenger,* in November 1917. Published until 1928, the *Messenger* became a highly respected black journal attracting some twenty-six thousand readers. In the *Messenger* Randolph and Owen expressed many controversial views, even leading to their brief arrest for expressing antiwar views in 1918 during World War I (1914–18). Their activity continued to expand. They organized the first black socialist organization in Harlem, the Friends of Negro Freedom, and unsuccessfully ran for local public offices.

Union leader

During the economic boom years of the 1920s, Randolph's radical political efforts lost their following. His attempts to organize black workers had limited success. However, in 1925 a group of porters invited Randolph to speak about trade unions. The Pullman Company employed the porters to provide services to railroad passengers. The porters asked Randolph to organize a union for them. On August 25, 1925, Randolph introduced The Brotherhood of Sleeping Car Porters at a mass meeting.

The Brotherhood soon rose in power as Randolph proved a very effective leader. In 1928 it was accepted into the American Federation of Labor (AFL), a national federation of labor unions representing various types of skilled craft workers. The arrival of the Great Depression (1929–41) in late 1929, however, set back the unions' effectiveness until 1933 when newly elected president **Franklin D. Roosevelt** (1882–1945; served 1933–45; see entry) signed into law legislation formally recognizing organized labor unions. In 1935 the Brotherhood became the first black union to gain formal recognition by industry. By 1937 it reached an agreement with Pullman over working conditions. The agreement brought an additional two million dollars in wages to the porters and greatly increased Randolph's national prestige.

In addition to his union activity, Randolph continued to press for social change, including racial equality for black Americans through economic progress. In 1935 Randolph became the first president of the newly created National Negro Congress (NNC). The NNC was a national organization designed to coordinate all existing black political groups in an effort to improve the economic condition of black America.

Wartime opportunities

In 1940 almost thirteen million black Americans lived in the United States. The mobilization of industry for war production beginning that year presented a new opportunity for economic improvement of black Americans. In addition, the Democratic Party pledged during the 1940 presidential campaign to work for civil rights in order to maintain the large black vote President Roosevelt received in 1936. However, disappointment soon returned. As industry began increasing its workers, the actual percentage of black workers in industry declined. Many industries sought only white workers.

Randolph and other black leaders decided it was time to take action, including public protests and mass demonstrations. In January 1941 Randolph called for a national march on Washington. In May plans were set for at least ten thousand black Americans to march on July 1. At the time, Roosevelt was trying to build national unity for the upcoming war effort. His predecessor, President Herbert Hoover (1874–1964; served 1929–33), experienced a public relations disaster in 1932 when thousands of World War I veterans marched on Washington wanting advanced payment of pay bonuses. The last thing Roosevelt wanted was another embarrassing march on Washington.

Yet Roosevelt on June 18 nominated Southern U.S. senator **James F. Byrnes** (1879–1972; see entry) to the Supreme Court despite strong protests from Randolph and others. The nomination further strained relations between the president and black leaders. Six days later Roosevelt met with Randolph and other black leaders, including Walter White of the National Association for the Advancement of Colored People (NAACP), to resolve their grievances so that the march could be called off. In the meeting were several governmental leaders besides Roosevelt, including secretary of war **Henry L. Stimson** (1867–1950; see entry). Roosevelt knew Randolph had the ability to stage the largest demonstration by black Americans in the nation's history. Randolph demanded an executive order from Roosevelt banning racial discrimination in hiring by war industries and integrating the armed forces. Roosevelt agreed to ban discrimination in war industries, but, with advice from Stimson, not to integrate the military. On the

Fair Employment Practices Committee

The Fair Employment Practices Committee (FEPC) was formed by President Franklin D. Roosevelt (1882–1945; served 1933–45) under pressure from black American leader A. Philip Randolph to ensure that the U.S. war industries did not discriminate in hiring workers. The FEPC bounced from agency to agency for its first two years. It began in 1941 in the Office of Production Management (OPM), then to the War Production Board (WPB), and on to the War Manpower Commission (WMC). Finally, in March 1943, Roosevelt placed the FEPC within the White House as part of the Office of Emergency Planning. U.S. senator James F. Byrnes (1879–1972), who was no friend of racial integration, assumed control over it. However, Byrnes directed most business related to the FEPC to another White House assistant, Jonathan Daniels (1902–1981). Daniels was Roosevelt's assistant on racial matters.

The FEPC held a series of public hearings in Los Angeles, California; Chicago, Illinois; Birmingham, Alabama; and New York City documenting instances of discrimination against blacks, Jews, and Mexican Americans in war industry hiring. Southerners accused the FEPC of spreading racial strife. As controversy increased, the administration called a halt to the hearings. By mid-1943 the FEPC was one of the most controversial agencies in wartime Washington. Southern Democrats in the U.S. House of Representatives opened hearings in 1944 to investigate certain agencies, with the FEPC being the first. It even became a major domestic campaign issue for the 1944 presidential elections.

Despite its limited powers, the FEPC served as a forum where black Americans could be heard and bring their work-related issues forward. The FEPC was abolished by Congress following the war, when military contracts to industry wound down.

following day, June 25, Roosevelt issued Executive Order 8802 requiring that all government contracts contain conditions prohibiting racial discrimination in the workplace. To carry out the plan, the order also created the Fair Employment Practice Committee (FEPC) with members appointed by the president. Randolph called off the march. It was a major victory for him. The executive order was the first major action by a U.S. president regarding equal rights since the 1870s, just after the American Civil War (1861–65). The executive order was also an affirmative action plan that preceded the 1960s affirmative action programs.

Controversy builds

The FEPC became one of the hottest controversies on the U.S. home front during the war. During the summer of 1943 a series of race riots occurred around the country. One of the earliest outbreaks resulted from an FEPC order directing the Alabama Dry Dock and Shipbuilding Company to promote some black Americans to skilled welding positions. White workers protested, leading to fights between segregated white and black work crews. Some eighty workers were injured before the Alabama National Guard restored order. Riots also occurred in Beaumont, Texas; Los Angeles, California; Philadelphia, Pennsylvania; and Harlem. The worst riot occurred on Sunday, June 20, in Detroit, Michigan. The FEPC claimed the main cause for the racial unrest was poor housing, recreation facilities, and public transportation available for minorities. However, others blamed the FEPC and its rulings for stirring up trouble. With progress in relieving racial discrimination largely nonexistent in 1943, Randolph again began threatening another march. He wanted Congress to make the FEPC a permanent agency with more stable funding and greater authority to enforce actions.

With the 1944 presidential election campaign approaching, Roosevelt had not yet given the FEPC his personal support. Southern Democrats were angry that he had gone too far. Black Americans, including Randolph, believed Roosevelt was far less supportive than he should be as the nation's leader. To resolve the matter, on November 4, 1943, Roosevelt voiced strong support for the FEPC, claiming its decisions were mandatory.

Nonetheless, Randolph, along with White and others, persisted with pressure. They signed a large newspaper advertisement calling for legislation creating a permanent FEPC. The black leaders were able to block James F. Byrnes from becoming Roosevelt's vice presidential running mate. Roosevelt won the unprecedented reelection to a fourth term partly owing to the black American vote he once again received.

A lasting influence

Following the war, Randolph pressed again to end segregation in the armed forces. He formed the League for Nonviolent Civil Disobedience Against Military Segregation.

Needing the black vote in the 1948 presidential election, President Harry S. Truman (1884–1972; served 1945–53) signed a presidential order ending racial segregation in the military in July 1948. It marked yet another major victory for Randolph.

In 1955 the AFL combined with the Congress of Industrial Organizations (CIO), a national union organization composed of semiskilled factory workers. Randolph was one of two blacks on the new AFL-CIO Executive Committee.

By the 1960s Randolph was widely recognized as an elder statesman of black America. Through World War II Randolph paved the way for the later civil rights movement of the 1950s and 1960s led by Martin Luther King Jr. (1929–1968). One of Randolph's biggest moments came on August 28, 1963, at seventy-four years of age. He was national director of the march on Washington, D.C., in which over two hundred thousand black and white Americans participated, seeking an end to racial discrimination. On the steps of the Lincoln Memorial,

A. Philip Randolph (at left) leads picketers in a protest to end racial segregation in the military outside the Democratic National Convention in Philadelphia, Pennsylvania, on July 12, 1948. © *Bettmann/Corbis. Reproduced by permission.*

Randolph delivered his last major public speech. He was followed at the podium by King, who delivered his epic "I Have a Dream" civil rights speech. As in 1941, the president—this time President John F. Kennedy (1917–1963; served 1961–63)—had tried to convince Randolph to call off the event. Although Randolph's wife died only three months before the march, Randolph decided the march must go on.

Much progress was realized after the historic march on Washington. The AFL-CIO adopted a strong national position in favor of the civil rights movement and lobbied for legislation prohibiting racial discrimination in the workplace. In 1964 Congress passed the landmark Civil Rights Act banning racial discrimination in public places. Also in 1964 Randolph established the A. Philip Randolph Institute to solve black labor issues and maintain ties between labor organizations and civil rights groups.

In 1968 Randolph was robbed and beaten outside his Harlem apartment building. Afterwards his health declined, leading him to resign as president of the Brotherhood of Sleeping Car Porters and from other labor positions. In 1971 Harvard University awarded Randolph an honorary degree. He died at the age of ninety in New York City on May 16, 1979. Randolph is remembered as a man of great integrity by both blacks and whites. In 1989 the U.S. Postal Service issued a Black Heritage Month stamp sporting his likeness.

For More Information

Books

Anderson, Jervis. *A. Philip Randolph: A Biographical Portrait.* New York: Harcourt Brace Jovanovich, 1973.

Davis, Daniel S. *Mr. Black Labor: The Story of A. Philip Randolph, Father of the Civil Rights Movement.* New York: E.P. Dutton, 1972.

Pfeiffer, Paula F. *A. Philip Randolph: Pioneer of the Civil Rights Movement.* Baton Rouge, LA: Louisiana State University Press, 1990.

Web sites

A. Philip Randolph Porter Museum. http://www.aphiliprandolphmuseum. com (accessed on July 24, 2004).

Norman Rockwell

Born February 3, 1894
New York, New York
Died November 8, 1978
Stockbridge, Massachusetts

Artist

Norman Rockwell was one of America's leading artists. He considered himself first and foremost an illustrator. Rockwell painted a great number of pictures for story illustrations, advertising campaigns, posters, calendars, and books. His long career spanned the days of horses and buggies to the days of space travel. The cover of the highly respected *The Saturday Evening Post* was his showcase for nearly fifty years.

Rockwell was taught that an illustration is an author's words in paint. He chose to tell the story of the American dream. The story he told, in great detail, was of a simpler time. He painted with warmth and humor and tapped into the nostalgia of the American people when life was uncertain. His paintings were often idyllic and expressed enthusiasm for the ordinary.

Early life

Norman Percevel Rockwell was born on February 3, 1894, at his family home just a few blocks west of Central Park in New York City. He was the second son born to J. Waring and

"Rockwell's practical sense of his own duty for World War II was to create images that would ensure the men and women fighting overseas got the . . . emotional support that sentimental images would ensure. . . ."

—From Norman Rockwell: A Life

Norman Rockwell.
© *Bettmann/Corbis.*
Reproduced by permission.

Nancy Hill Rockwell. His elder brother, Jarvis, was the athlete in the family. Young Norman found he could compensate for his own lack of athleticism by drawing for his friends. Norman picked up the basics of sketching from his father, and it was the one skill for which he was recognized. It was common for the two of them to spend an evening copying simple scenes from one of the weekly magazines that came to the house. Waring Rockwell had no artistic ambitions of his own and was content to serve out his career as a branch office manager for a cotton textile mill. Norman's Grandfather Hill was an impoverished artist who had immigrated to America from England. He was a painter of portraits and landscapes by preference, occasionally a house painter by necessity. Hill never achieved professional success, but Norman was fascinated by some of his grandfather's paintings, particularly their close attention to detail.

The Rockwell family moved to suburban Mamaroneck, New York, in 1903, where Norman's father continued the custom of reading aloud to the family as they gathered around the dining room table before bedtime. Charles Dickens (1812–1870) was a favorite author and Norman would sketch the characters he visualized while his father's mellow baritone described them. Norman ceased to merely copy others' work and began using his imagination to create new pictures of his own.

High school

During his freshman year at Mamaroneck High, Norman decided to take his drawing seriously and become an illustrator. He used the few dollars he earned at odd chores to pay for lessons at an accredited art school. Every Wednesday and Saturday he would take the two-hour subway ride to New York City to attend classes at the Chase School of Fine and Applied Art.

At fifteen, in the middle of his sophomore year, Norman left high school to study full time at the National Academy of Design and then at the Art Students League, both in New York City, under George Bridgman and Thomas Fogarty. He was a diligent student whose hard work and sense of humor were widely recognized.

Major breakthrough

In 1912 Norman Rockwell had his first book illustrating job, for C. H. Claudy's *Tell Me Why: Stories about Mother Nature.* By 1913, at the age of nineteen, he was art editor for *Boys' Life,* the official magazine for the Boy Scouts of America. Known as the "Boy Illustrator," Rockwell worked for several years illustrating for a wide variety of young people's magazines.

In 1916 Rockwell crossed over to an adult audience when he received a commission to paint a cover for *The Saturday Evening Post.* It was to be the first of more than three hundred paintings he would illustrate for the highly acclaimed magazine. With his windfall earnings boosting his confidence, Norman proposed marriage to girlfriend Irene O'Connor. They were married that fall and settled into their new home in New Rochelle, New York.

Rockwell continued to use children as his principal subject matter, but he looked at them in a different way. He now attempted to amuse adults with the antics of kids and evoke nostalgia for the pleasures of childhood. He painted them from the adult viewpoint, which sees childhood as a carefree and uncomplicated time.

The world at war

Six months after Rockwell's marriage, in April 1917, President Woodrow Wilson (1856–1924; served 1913–21) signed a proclamation that a state of war existed between the United States and the imperial government of Germany. Fired with idealism, Rockwell enlisted in the navy with dreams of becoming a hero for his country. Severely underweight, the new recruit was assigned to the Charleston Navy Yard and put to work as an artist on the camp newspaper, *Afloat and Ashore.* Left with a great deal of time on his hands, Rockwell continued his career as a magazine illustrator and turned out many paintings for the *Post* and other magazines, often making more money than an admiral.

The war ended in November 1918, and Rockwell received an early, special discharge after painting a portrait of his commanding officer. Work poured in for the young artist, making him both rich and famous. The 1920s was the Jazz Age and a boom period in American living. Rockwell had the

Thornton Oakley

While Norman Rockwell painted people, Thornton Oakley (1881–1953) was known for his paintings of industrial America. Oakley graduated with a degree in architecture from the University of Pennsylvania and then studied art under renowned artist Howard Pyle (1853–1911), founder of the Brandywine School, in Wilmington, Delaware.

Thornton Oakley married Amy Ewing in 1910, and together they published numerous travel books, which she wrote and he illustrated. During World War II (1939–45), the National Geographic Society commissioned forty-eight paintings of war plants and related topics from Oakley. To fulfill his assignment, the artist traveled from coast to coast and visited steel mills, grain elevators, shipyards, chemical plants, assembly lines, oil refineries, and more. His paintings, as well as his written reflections, appeared in the December 1942 issue of *The National Geographic Magazine* titled "American Industries Geared for War." Oakley used his canvases to vividly portray the highlights of America's vast war production effort.

Oakley's next assignment with National Geographic was to do a series on transportation titled "America Transportation Vital to Victory." He was to capture the spirit of America's might in moving men, materials, and supplies. Once again he was on the road for months to cover everything from railroads to cargo planes, from highways to tankers. His impressive paintings appeared in the December 1943 issue of *The National Geographic Magazine* and were accompanied once again by his patriotic and descriptive writings.

opportunity to travel to Europe and South America, and the Rockwells were popular guests in society circles. In 1926 Rockwell painted the first *Post* cover ever produced in full color. By 1929 the economy had crashed and so had the Rockwell marriage.

A new beginning

In 1930 Rockwell married Mary Rhodes Barstow. Their first son was born in 1932, and two others followed by 1936. Rockwell became the illustrator for one of his favorite authors, Mark Twain (1835–1910). He was asked to illustrate both *Tom Sawyer* and *Huckleberry Finn*. Recording the trivial events in the lives of two ordinary American boys was a perfect fit for Rockwell.

THE SATURDAY EVENING POST

MAY 29, 1943   10¢

BEGINNING—A NEW
KELLAND SERIAL
Heart on Her Sleeve

EDGAR SNOW
REPORTS ON GERMAN
ATROCITIES

Cover illustration for the May 29, 1943 *Saturday Evening Post* depicting "Rosie the Riveter." This painting was one of many that Norman Rockwell created to inspire Americans to support the war effort. *Reprinted by permission of the Norman Rockwell Family Agency. Copyright © 1943 the Norman Rockwell Family Entities.*

In 1939 Rockwell moved his family to a farm in Arlington, Vermont. It was an ideal place for Norman and Mary to raise their three boys. Their new neighbors were wonderful models for Rockwell, and he continued his practice of painting every day except Christmas, when he would work only a half-day.

The early 1940s were years of change, even for a quiet community like Arlington. An increasing number of young men from the town were joining the armed forces. Then World War II began in earnest. Rockwell was interested in telling the story of the boys next door who had become the boys in uniform. His idea was to follow the path of a typical rookie in the war effort. The character was called Willie Gillis, and he appeared on magazine covers frequently in a series of whimsical scenes. The series ended abruptly when the young model Rockwell had "drafted" from the local Grange Hall enlisted as a naval aviator and left for an overseas assignment.

The "Four Freedoms"

Rockwell looked for a way to make a personal contribution to the war effort. He painted a variety of covers, including the famous "Rosie the Riveter" for the *Post*. Rockwell did not like to glorify killing, so the only battle picture he ever painted was for the army's ordnance department. It was a dramatic poster that showed a machine gunner, his uniform in shreds, in what appeared to be a tough spot on the firing line. The coil of cartridge tape and the empty cartridges showed that he was about down to his last shot. The caption read, "Let's give him enough and on time." Through his paintings, Rockwell was looking for a way to explain to the home front what America was fighting for to evoke a response of patriotism. These paintings were not done to amuse or entertain; their purpose was to inspire.

On January 6, 1941, President **Franklin D. Roosevelt** (1882–1945; served 1933–45; see entry) delivered his annual State of the Union address to the Seventy-seventh Congress of the United States. One particular passage, as found in *The Public Papers and Addresses of Franklin D. Roosevelt, 1940 Volume,* and which became popularly known as the "Four Freedoms," sparked inspiration in Rockwell:

> *In the future days which we seek to make secure, we look forward to a world founded upon four essential human freedoms. The first is freedom of speech and expression—everywhere in the world. The second is freedom of every person to worship God in his own way—everywhere in the world. The third is freedom from want, which, translated into world terms, means economic understandings which will secure to every nation a healthy peacetime life for its inhabitants—everywhere in the world. The fourth is freedom from fear, which, translated into world terms, means a world-wide reduction of armaments to such a point and in such a thorough fashion that no nation will be in a position to commit an act of physical aggression against any neighbor—anywhere in the world.*

OURS...to fight for

FREEDOM FROM WANT

Rockwell was so inspired by the speech that he offered to create a series of paintings on the "Four Freedoms" free of charge. The government rejected his offer, but *The Saturday Evening Post* commissioned the paintings for its magazine. They were to be full-page illustrations inside the magazine, accompanied by an article on each of the four freedoms. Rockwell would interpret each of the four using his own Vermont neighbors exercising those freedoms in their homes, churches, and town meetings. His genius of simplification reduced each freedom to an easily understood metaphor (an image that represents the meaning) while the world was reeling from the threat of their loss.

After ten painstaking months the four canvases were delivered. The response was overwhelming. Requests came in for millions of reprints. The U.S. government soon adopted them for use during World War II. War bond shows were held in sixteen cities, where the paintings drew crowds of more than a million people who bought over $133,000,000 in bonds. The paintings' popularity was considered an important part of the home front war effort.

Disaster strikes

In the spring of 1943 Rockwell's studio burned to the ground, and he lost his life's work. Fortunately, he had shipped "Freedom of Worship" to Philadelphia several days earlier or it, too, would have been lost. Mary and Norman now had a tough decision to make. They decided it was a good time to move, and they found a place they liked several miles away in West Arlington. Rockwell immediately began work on a new studio. This one had fire extinguishers and a sprinkler system.

When the war ended, Rockwell went back to painting his neighbors as well as presidential candidates and movie stars. The Rockwell children were all in college, so in 1953 Mary and Norman made another move, this time to Stockbridge, Massachusetts. The 1950s saw a series of presidential candidates being committed to canvas, but the decade ended tragically in 1959 with the death of Norman's beloved wife, Mary.

In 1960 Rockwell turned once again to a serious subject. Concerned about the growing nuclear arms race between the two world superpowers of the United States and the Soviet Union, known as the Cold War (1945–91), he searched for a way to contribute and decided he would paint "The Golden Rule—Do unto Others as You Would Have Them Do unto You." Rockwell remembered a ten-foot-long, unfinished charcoal drawing of his United Nations picture and turned to it for inspiration. For the next five months he worked to tell the story with greater impact. The finished work graced the April 1, 1961, cover of *The Saturday Evening*

Post and was received with international acclaim. The painting shows a crowded group of people of various nationalities and ages, from the very old to the very young, all of whose facial expressions are focused and expectant as if toward a common goal for the betterment of mankind. Realizing the international relations value of Rockwell's painting, the U.S. State Department produced a thirty-minute film on Rockwell and the painting. It was translated into seventy languages for showing abroad.

At the end of May 1961, the former high school dropout was invited to the University of Massachusetts to receive an honorary degree of Doctor of Fine Arts.

Looking forward

Rockwell met and married Mary L. (Molly) Punderson in 1961, and the two traveled extensively around the globe. Prompted by Molly, new markets, and the changing times, Rockwell used his art to cover a wide range of social issues in the 1970s. In addition to civil rights and poverty, he addressed the Peace Corps and the Space Age.

Norman Rockwell died on November 8, 1978, at the age of eighty-four. In his 1978 book *A Rockwell Portrait: An Intimate Biography,* author Donald Walton asked Rockwell about the secret to his longevity. Walton stated that Rockwell mused, "Well, maybe the secret to so many artists living so long is that every painting is a new adventure. So, you see, they're always *looking ahead* to something new and exciting. The secret is not to look back."

For More Information

Books

Buechner, Thomas S. *Norman Rockwell: Artist and Illustrator.* New York: Harry N. Abrams, 1970.

Claridge, Laura. *Norman Rockwell: A Life.* New York: Random House, 2001.

Guptill, Arthur L. *Norman Rockwell—Illustrator.* New York: Watson-Guptill Publications, 1946.

Rockwell, Norman. *The Norman Rockwell Album.* Garden City, NY: Doubleday, 1961.

Roosevelt, Franklin D. *The Public Papers and Addresses of Franklin D. Roosevelt, 1940 Volume.* New York: Macmillan, 1941.

Walton, Donald. *A Rockwell Portrait: An Intimate Biography.* Kansas City, KS: Sheed Andrews and McMeel, 1978.

Periodicals

Oakley, Thornton. "American Industries Geared for War." *The National Geographic Magazine* (December 1942): pp. 716–34.

Oakley, Thornton. "American Transportation Vital to Victory." *The National Geographic Magazine* (December 1943): pp. 671–88.

Web sites

"American Masters—Norman Rockwell." *Public Broadcasting System.* http://www.pbs.org/wnet/americanmasters/database/rockwell_n.html (accessed on July 25, 2004).

"The Art of Norman Rockwell." *The Norman Rockwell Museum at Stockbridge.* http://www.nrm.org/exhibits/current/four-freedoms.html (accessed on July 25, 2004).

"Thornton Oakley Diaries." *The University of Delaware Library.* http://www.lib.udel.edu/ud/spec/findaids/oakley.htm (accessed on July 25, 2004).

Eleanor Roosevelt

Born October 11, 1884
New York, New York
Died November 7, 1962
Hyde Park, New York

First lady of the United States,
social activist

Eleanor Roosevelt served as first lady from March 1933 to April 1945, longer than any other president's wife. She also was one of the first first ladies to work tirelessly for social reforms both in the United States and worldwide. Checking on conditions throughout the nation during World War II (1939–45) and earlier, she was President **Franklin D. Roosevelt**'s (1882–1945; served 1933–45; see entry) "eyes and ears." During the war years, she advocated for improved employment opportunities for women and minorities and helped her husband give comfort to the nation during the times of crisis.

"Few Americans . . . were neutral in their feelings about this powerful woman who refused to accept the traditional role of a president's wife."

—*From* No Ordinary Time: Franklin and Eleanor Roosevelt, the Home Front in World War II

Early childhood lessons

Anna Eleanor Roosevelt was born on October 11, 1884, in New York City to Elliott Roosevelt and Anna Hall Roosevelt. She had two younger brothers. Both of her parents were from wealthy, prominent families in New York society. Elliott's older brother Theodore Roosevelt (1858–1919; served 1901–09) became president of the United States in 1901. Anna was beautiful, charming, and very popular within the social world.

Eleanor Roosevelt.
© *Bettmann/Corbis.*
Reproduced by permission.

Anna was dismayed with her young daughter's plain appearance and often called her "granny," to Eleanor's embarrassment. Elliott had a drinking problem. In December 1892, when Eleanor was only eight years old, Anna contracted diphtheria and suddenly died. Eleanor and her two younger brothers, Elliott and Hall, went to her maternal grandmother's home in New York City. That winter the youngest brother, Elliott, also died of diphtheria. Tragedy struck again in August 1894 when Eleanor's father died.

Little warmth existed in Eleanor's childhood. She was raised by her grandmother more out of duty than love. From her childhood, Eleanor learned that love and approval were hard to find and not likely to last. The resulting feeling of self-doubt would pursue her all her life. Eleanor found great joy in helping others, which gave her a sense of purpose and usefulness.

A calling to social service

In 1899 at the age of fifteen, Eleanor was enrolled in Allenswood, a school near London, England. French headmistress Marie Souvestre, a strong, liberal-minded woman, liked Eleanor and took her along on travels through Europe during school breaks. Souvestre taught Eleanor about the world of art, encouraged her to think for herself, and stressed service to the less fortunate. This experience would have a lasting effect on Eleanor.

At eighteen, Eleanor returned to New York in 1902 to enter the New York social scene. However, she also began social work that winter, joining the National Consumer's League, which promoted worker safety and taught children of immigrants at a house for the poor, the Rivington Street Settlement House. Later in 1902, Eleanor's distant cousin Franklin Delano Roosevelt began courting her. They would see each other on various occasions such as parties at his Hyde Park home and at White House events. They married just over two years later in March 1905. Her uncle, President Theodore Roosevelt, gave Eleanor away. Eleanor and Franklin first lived in a small apartment in New York City while Franklin attended Columbia Law School. They would have one daughter and four sons.

Eleanor and Franklin

Eleanor's mother-in-law, Sara Delano Roosevelt, had a very domineering personality. Sara insisted that Eleanor drop her social activism and become a young society matron dependent on others. Eleanor would increasingly resent her intrusion in their lives as the years went by.

Eleanor's first experience in politics came in 1911, when Franklin won election to a seat in the New York State Senate. Two years later, she and Franklin moved to Washington, D.C., when he was appointed assistant secretary of the navy by President Woodrow Wilson (1856–1924; served 1913–21). Though Franklin enjoyed the Washington social life, Eleanor at first found it meaningless.

When the United States entered World War I (1914–18) in April 1917, Eleanor was able to resume volunteer work. She helped operate a Red Cross canteen and tended to navy wounded. She also helped organize the Navy Red Cross. As the war came to an end in November 1918, Eleanor's personal life seemingly fell apart. She discovered Franklin had fallen in love with her own young and beautiful personal secretary, Lucy Mercer. Franklin promised never to see Lucy again, but Eleanor's self-pride and confidence suffered. Out of her marital crisis Eleanor launched a more determined career in social reform and political activism.

Franklin resigned his naval post in 1920 to be the vice presidential running mate of James M. Cox. Though they lost badly, Franklin's campaign abilities proved extremely popular with Democrats. The campaign also put Eleanor in the national spotlight. They returned to New York City and Franklin formed a law partnership.

In the summer of 1921, another tragedy came to the family when Franklin became ill with polio-like symptoms that included paralysis of his legs. For the next seven years, while pursuing her own causes, Eleanor and others kept Franklin informed on political issues. During Franklin's lengthy recuperation, Eleanor served as his "legs and eyes." During the 1920s Eleanor became a leader in four New York groups: the League of Women Voters, the Women's City Club, the Women's Trade Union League, and the Women's Division of the New York State Democratic Committee. The City Club and Trade Union League sought social reform, particularly better working conditions for women. Through these organizations, Eleanor developed friendships with many women activists who would be influential throughout the remainder of her political life.

In 1926 Franklin planned and had built for Eleanor a cottage, called Val-Kill, on the Hyde Park property. At Val-Kill Eleanor operated an Early American furniture manufacturing company with two friends. Also, the threesome bought Todhunter School in New York City, a private school for girls. Eleanor began teaching there in 1927 in several subjects including American history, English, literature, and current events. Eleanor also began making political speeches on her own and continued to relay to the improving Franklin the thinking on various issues. Franklin would rely on Eleanor in this way for the rest of his life.

Recovered such that he could walk with the aid of heavy braces and a cane, Franklin won the 1928 governor's race for New York. The Roosevelts moved to Albany, New York's capital, but Eleanor continued to teach two and a half days a week in New York City.

First lady

In 1932 Franklin handily won the presidential election. The nation was at the depth of the Great Depression (1929–41). Beginning in the fall of 1929, the Great Depression was the worst economic crisis in U.S. history. Approximately 25 percent of the nation's workforce was unemployed, and many Americans did not have enough food. In this time of national need, Eleanor set the standard for first lady social involvement against which future first ladies would be measured. Even further, she became a role model for women actively involved in their communities and nation.

Eleanor believed government had the responsibility to aid those people struggling most. She made sure that people who do not normally have access to the president, such as women, youth, blue-collar workers, and black Americans, gained his attention. Eleanor's energy and tireless work became legendary. Eleanor pressed for appointments of women to high government positions and for women in general to benefit from government programs. She supported federal antilynching

Office of Civilian Defense Controversy

Eleanor Roosevelt was very busy during the war trying to keep morale high on the home front and pursuing rights for women and minorities. For five months, beginning in September 1941, she also served as assistant national director for the Office of Civilian Defense (OCD). It was the first government position ever held by a first lady in U.S. history. Roosevelt worked with the OCD director, **Fiorello La Guardia** (1882–1947; see entry), to support a wide range of home front volunteer programs in support of the war effort. While La Guardia focused primarily on air raid warning systems, Roosevelt sought to include social services such as nursery schools, recreation centers, and homes for the aged in OCD. These efforts by Roosevelt attracted considerable criticism from the media and Congress. Roosevelt's hiring of a close friend to teach dancing to children was finally the last straw for the critics. Congress even began withholding funds from OCD. The criticism increased to such an extent that Roosevelt finally concluded the mission of OCD was being jeopardized by her involvement. In addition, she and La Guardia were suffering from a conflict in personalities. In February 1942 both she and La Guardia stepped down from their OCD duties. President Franklin D. Roosevelt (1882–1945; served 1933–45) restored calm to the agency with new leadership.

laws that her husband would not endorse for fear of losing Southern votes.

A source of advice and information

From 1933 to 1945 Eleanor would write or dictate thousands of newspaper and magazine articles, publish six books, make numerous speeches, travel thousands of miles, and hold weekly press conferences. Her weekly press conferences were for women journalists only. Media organizations had to employ women reporters on their staff in Washington, D.C. One effect was that it led to national news from a woman's point of view. Thousands of individuals wrote personal letters to Eleanor about their troubles. She often passed requests on to the appropriate agency and personally answered many letters.

At first Eleanor wrote a weekly column for the *Women's Home Companion,* but she began writing "My Day," which became a syndicated daily column in January 1936. The column continued until her death in 1962. With war developing in early 1941, Eleanor wrote a monthly question-and-answer column, "If You Ask Me," for *Ladies' Home Journal* from June 1941 to the spring of 1949 and for *McCall's* from 1949 until her death. Between the years 1933 and 1945 alone, it is estimated she wrote twenty-five hundred newspaper columns and three hundred magazine articles.

In her articles and public appearances during the war, Eleanor answered questions on a wide range of topics, including prospects for continued employment of women after the war, postwar educational opportunities for servicemen, the condition of servicemen overseas following her journeys, women's issues in the service, the conduct of war in China, service allowances for wives of soldiers, various military policies, and rationing.

A spokeswoman for the common person

During the war, Eleanor often boldly spoke out in favor of unpopular issues on the home front. For example, she strongly supported the Fair Employment Practices Commission (FEPC) that promoted fairness in the hiring of black Americans and other minorities in the war industries. Despite the criticism directed at Eleanor for her public support, particularly from the South, President Roosevelt never publicly objected to her position on this issue.

Eleanor also took a position supporting the draft of individuals, including women, to work in war industries. By late in 1942 workforce shortages were appearing. Eleanor and others argued that some form of government control was needed to ensure critical war industries had a sufficient and stable workforce. The public opposed Eleanor's position and her husband did as well. The home front draft was never instituted.

America's wartime ambassador

With Franklin hampered by his physical disabilities and busy with the conduct of World War II (1939–45), Eleanor served as his personal ambassador to other nations. Eleanor

received numerous foreign visitors at the White House, often from countries looking for U.S. assistance.

Eleanor also took extensive trips at home and abroad. For example, after touring the United States in September 1942 with Franklin inspecting war factories, military camps, and navy shipyards, Eleanor left for Britain in October. Queen Elizabeth (1900–2002) had invited her to see the types of work the women were doing to assist in Britain's war effort and to visit U.S. servicemen stationed there. The following year Eleanor journeyed to the Pacific front, including the South Pacific islands, New Zealand, and Australia. Supporting the American Red Cross, she visited numerous hospital wards where U.S. servicemen were recovering physically and emotionally from severe injuries. In March 1944 she took a thirteen thousand-mile trip to the Caribbean, where U.S. servicemen were stationed, and on to Central and South America.

In April 1945 as the war was winding down, Franklin went to his retreat at Warm Springs, Georgia, for a rest. On the

Eleanor Roosevelt often served as her husband Franklin's personal ambassador to other countries during his presidency. Here, Oveta Culp Hobby (center-left), and Eleanor Roosevelt (center-right) visit U.S. servicemen in England, October 26, 1942.
Courtesy of the FDR Library.

afternoon of April 12 he collapsed from a cerebral hemorrhage (bleeding in the brain) and died. It was a time of shock and sorrow for the Roosevelt family as well as for the nation.

Serving the postwar world

Eleanor quickly moved from the White House to her Val-Kill cottage. She also maintained an apartment overlooking Washington Square in New York City. She turned the large family house at Hyde Park over to the U.S. government for safekeeping. World War II would end only a few months later. Eleanor regretted that Franklin did not live long enough to enjoy watching the celebrations.

The following year, in 1946, President Harry S. Truman (1884–1972; served 1945–53) appointed Eleanor Roosevelt as a delegate to the United Nations (UN) General Assembly. The UN delegates elected Roosevelt chairman of the UN's Human Rights Commission. In that position she helped author the Universal Declaration of Human Rights, a major worldwide statement of the basic rights of individuals. Roosevelt thoroughly enjoyed her time as a UN delegate traveling throughout the world for humanitarian causes, visiting the Arab countries, Israel, Pakistan, and India. She left the UN in 1953 when Republican Dwight D. Eisenhower (1890–1969; served 1953–61) moved into the White House as president. Following her departure from the UN, Roosevelt traveled as a volunteer for the American Association for the United Nations (AAUN), which promoted the need and work of the UN. She traveled to Japan, Hong Kong, Turkey, Greece, and Yugoslavia. In 1957 and 1958 Eleanor traveled to the Soviet Union, meeting with Soviet leader Nikita Khrushchev (1894–1971).

A full life

After leaving the UN, Roosevelt continued writing her regular newspaper column, published three times a week since 1935. She also wrote a monthly *McCall's* magazine page, did radio and television work, lectured widely, and served as a volunteer member of the AAUN.

A steady stream of dignitaries, family, and friends made their way to Hyde Park during Roosevelt's last years to pay respects and gain her insights on issues. She also campaigned for various Democratic Party political candidates. Knowing her health was fading, in February 1962 Roosevelt made her last trip to Europe. She died later that year on November 7, 1962, at Val-Kill of a rare ailment, bone-marrow tuberculosis.

For More Information

Books

Freedman, Russell. *Eleanor Roosevelt: A Life of Discovery.* New York: New Clarion Books, 1993.

Goodwin, Doris Kearns. *No Ordinary Time: Franklin and Eleanor Roosevelt, the Home Front in World War II.* New York: Simon & Schuster, 1994.

Hareven, Tamara R. *Eleanor Roosevelt: An American Conscience.* Chicago: Quadrangle Books, 1968.

Roosevelt, David B. *Grandmere: A Personal History of Eleanor Roosevelt.* New York: Warnerbooks, 2002.

Roosevelt, Eleanor. *The Autobiography of Eleanor Roosevelt.* New York: Harper & Brothers Publishers, 1961.

Skarmeas, Nancy J., ed. *Eleanor Roosevelt: A Photobiography.* Nashville, TN: Ideals Publications, 1997.

Winget, Mary. *Eleanor Roosevelt.* Minneapolis: Lerner Publications, 2003.

Franklin D. Roosevelt

Born January 30, 1882
Hyde Park, New York
Died April 12, 1945
Warm Springs, Georgia

**Thirty-second president of
the United States**

> "I have never known a
> man who gave one a
> greater sense of
> security. . . . [H]e believed
> in the courage and ability
> of men, and they
> responded."
>
> —*Eleanor Roosevelt*

Franklin D. Roosevelt.
The Library of Congress.

Franklin D. Roosevelt, commonly referred to as FDR, was the thirty-second president of the United States. Largely owing to the home front uncertainties of World War II (1939–45), Roosevelt is the only U.S. president to have been elected four times. Roosevelt entered the White House in March 1933 at the height of the Great Depression (1929–41). The Great Depression, which began in the fall of 1929, was the worst economic crisis in U.S. history. Approximately 25 percent of the nation's workforce was unemployed as business activity dramatically slowed, and many Americans did not have enough food. Roosevelt's charm, broad grin, and willingness to surround himself with able advisors brought hope to most Americans, first during the Depression and then through the war. Through his years as president, Roosevelt greatly expanded the powers of the federal government and reshaped the Democratic Party. To many in the United States and throughout the world, Roosevelt was the savior of democracy by defeating the Axis powers (Germany, Italy, and Japan) and restoring the U.S. economy. Roosevelt had an incredible ability to mobilize the nation in times of crisis and maintain a high level of public support during trying times.

A privileged upbringing

An only child, Franklin Delano Roosevelt was born to James and Sara Delano Roosevelt on January 30, 1882. The family was wealthy and lived on their Hyde Park estate in the Hudson River Valley of Dutchess County, New York. Their ancestors had accumulated the wealth from maritime trade in the early nineteenth century. Through his early school years young Franklin was privately tutored, both at home and on the family's frequent European travels. A major change came in Franklin's life in 1891 when his father suffered the first in a series of heart attacks, leaving him largely incapacitated. Young Franklin learned to hide his emotions, always presenting a calm and cheerful appearance to his frail father. This manner would be one of his greatest personal assets later in life while leading the nation through the Depression and war.

In 1896 at fourteen years of age, Franklin left home to attend Groton Preparatory School, a Massachusetts boarding school. It was the first time for Franklin to attend school with others his age. Though feeling very awkward socially, Franklin was greatly influenced by the Groton experience, which reinforced the family Episcopal values of a civic duty to serve the less fortunate. Through Groton, Franklin performed religious and charity work at places such as a boys club in Boston.

Franklin Roosevelt entered Harvard in 1900. His father died during his first year and his mother moved to Boston to be near him. At Harvard his social life flourished as he assumed many extracurricular activities, including president of the Harvard student newspaper. He also became more seriously interested in politics, particularly the progressive movement led by his distant cousin Theodore Roosevelt (1858–1919; served 1901–09), who was elected vice president in 1900. Progressivism called for an increased role of government in solving the nation's social and economic problems. Theodore became president in September 1901 following the assassination of President William McKinley (1843–1901; served 1897–1901). Franklin Roosevelt's buoyant personality and outward self-assurance gave him a persuasive but nonthreatening manner with others. A future trademark of Roosevelt's public speaking was his genial greeting, "My friends."

Theodore's niece, **Eleanor Roosevelt** (1884–1962; see entry), also caught Franklin's attention. Eleanor was active in New York City charities serving the poor. The two distant cousins increasingly saw each other through the next few years, including at White House events. Outwardly they seemed opposite in personality. Eleanor was very serious and reserved. However, they shared intelligence and a compassion for others. Franklin graduated from Harvard in 1904 and married Eleanor in March 1905. Theodore gave Eleanor away in the wedding. Franklin and Eleanor had four sons and a daughter.

Early politics and the navy

Franklin Roosevelt entered Columbia Law School in 1905. Though not receiving a degree, he passed New York's bar exam and began work as a law clerk for a prestigious Wall Street law firm in New York City. Roosevelt's strong interest in public service was known to the Democratic Party leaders of Dutchess County. They invited him to run for the state senate in 1910. At twenty-eight years of age, Roosevelt surprisingly won the election. An advocate for an open and honest government at a time when political corruption was dominant in New York politics, Roosevelt easily won reelection in 1912.

In early 1913 newly elected President Woodrow Wilson (1856–1924; served 1913–21), a democrat, appointed Roosevelt assistant secretary of the navy, a position Theodore Roosevelt had earlier held in his rise to the presidency. Franklin loved the Washington, D.C., atmosphere, and made a name for himself by personally resolving naval shipyard labor issues involving unions and the navy's civilian workers. Roosevelt ran for the U.S. Senate in 1914, but was unsuccessful. When the United States entered World War I (1914–18) in 1917, Roosevelt held an important position overseeing naval operations in the North Atlantic. It was during this time, in 1918, that his relationship with Eleanor took a different course. She discovered a romantic relationship between Franklin and her personal secretary, Lucy Mercer. They remained married, but their relationship became less intimate and based more on shared political goals and a mutual respect for each other.

A rising political star

After seven years as assistant secretary of the navy, Roosevelt in 1920 was selected vice presidential running mate for Ohio governor James M. Cox (1870–1957). Roosevelt resigned his naval post for the campaign. Though they soundly lost, Roosevelt showed strong campaigning skills and made many new influential friends.

Roosevelt's life took another dramatic change in August 1921 when he became ill with polio-like symptoms. Within only a few days his legs were paralyzed. Given no hope of walking again, Roosevelt retreated to the family's Hyde Park estate for the next seven years to recover while desperately hoping for a cure. While trying various forms of therapy he discovered spa-like baths in Warm Springs, Georgia. Roosevelt bought an old resort hotel at Warm Springs and transformed it into a center for treating polio victims. Through time, Roosevelt learned how to conceal his paralysis from the public. He would wear heavy leg braces and support himself with a cane and the arm of another person, often one of his sons. Throughout the rest of his life the media very quietly cooperated in not reporting his disability. Few photographs were taken of him in a wheelchair. As a result, the public knew little of his confinement to a wheelchair when not in public view. The experience gave him even greater sympathy for those who suffered in life.

A triumphant comeback

While Roosevelt was rebuilding his strength, Eleanor and others kept his political career alive. Eleanor made many public appearances, and her husband on occasion made speeches at Democratic national meetings. Ready for a return in 1928, Roosevelt successfully won the New York governorship. Tackling the serious economic issues of the early Great Depression years in the populous state, Roosevelt proved very popular. His landslide reelection victory in 1930 made him a favorite for the next Democratic presidential candidate for 1932.

During the 1932 presidential campaign, Roosevelt's charm and broad grin sharply contrasted with President Herbert Hoover's (1874–1964; served 1929–33) stern manner.

As a result, Roosevelt easily won the election. Roosevelt's calm, reassuring manner was put to a test in February 1933 when a lone gunman made an assassination attempt on his life in Miami, Florida. Roosevelt escaped injury, and his aides were awestruck by his seemingly unperturbed manner as the city's mayor, who was shot instead of Roosevelt, lay dying in his arms as they were rushed away from the shooting scene to the hospital.

Establishing a calm

Roosevelt entered the White House in March 1933 at the depth of the worst economic crisis in U.S. history. Most banks were closed, thirteen million workers were unemployed, and industrial production had fallen 44 percent from its 1929 levels. The nation was in turmoil. As he would during World War II, Roosevelt casually spoke directly to the nation through a series of radio addresses, called "Fireside Chats," on important issues, explaining why he was taking certain actions. He used his calm, friendly voice and simple language. With calm soon restored to a worried nation, Roosevelt established one landmark economic and social program after another, collectively known as the New Deal, reshaping the U.S. government.

Roosevelt's popularity soared as a broad coalition of voters including black Americans, farmers, the poor, women, and the working class, in addition to traditional liberals and progressives, came together to support his reelection in 1936. Roosevelt won by a landslide. This newly formed Democratic Coalition would propel Democratic candidates for decades to come.

Supporting Britain

Despite his popularity, by late 1937 Roosevelt's grip on Congress lessened. A growing coalition of conservative Republicans and Southern Democrats in Congress began blocking further reform legislation proposed by Roosevelt. In addition, international events were gaining greater attention from Roosevelt. With the rise of military dictatorships in Germany, Japan, and Italy, the threat of war was steadily growing in both Europe and Asia. The general public and Congress

Atlantic Charter

As late as August 1941, President Franklin D. Roosevelt was still dealing with an American public and Congress reluctant to become entangled in the war raging in Europe. The president had to convince the home front about the need to at least help Britain and perhaps even enter the war itself. On August 14 Roosevelt met with British leader Winston Churchill (1874–1965) for five days on warships in the North Atlantic off the Newfoundland coast of Canada. Together they identified the goals for going to war against Nazi Germany. These goals were captured in a document known as the Atlantic Charter.

In the Charter, the two leaders declared that all nations should live safely within their own borders, free from outside threat, that no changes in national boundaries should occur without approval of those living within the affected areas, that citizens have the right to choose their own form of government, and that the high seas should be safe for trade and travel. Any aggressor nation posing a threat should be disarmed. They went further to proclaim that global cooperation should seek to raise labor standards, increase the social security of the general population, and promote international trade. Regarding war, they also affirmed that the United States and Great Britain were not seeking increased power or wealth.

The Charter, reflecting the war aims identified by Roosevelt in his famous "Four Freedoms" speech to the American public in January 1941, directly influenced the Declaration of United Nations signed by twenty-six nations on January 1, 1942, shortly after the United States formally entered the war. The surprise Japanese attack on Pearl Harbor, Hawaii, in December 1941 finally rallied the home front fully behind Roosevelt. However, most Americans went to war simply to defend life as they knew it in their home front community and not to promote the ideals of the Atlantic Charter.

still held a strong mood of isolationism (avoiding foreign commitments or involvement) since World War I. Roosevelt therefore had to very cautiously develop foreign policy. Following Germany's invasion of Poland in September 1939, Britain and France declared war on Germany. World War II had begun. While voicing a neutral position to please the public, Roosevelt clearly supported Britain and its allies.

In the fall of 1939 Roosevelt had Congress repeal the Neutrality Acts that had banned the United States from selling weapons and supplies to foreign countries. He then initiated a "cash and carry" program in which Britain paid cash for war materials and had to carry them back to Britain in their own ships. In the spring of 1940 German military forces swept into Western Europe, eventually capturing Paris, France, in June. The U.S. public mood shifted more toward Roosevelt's perspective. In September 1940 Roosevelt traded fifty aging destroyers to Britain for seven military bases in the Caribbean. In November 1940 Roosevelt won an unprecedented reelection to a third presidential term. His victory largely resulted from the public's fear of what was coming. They wanted to keep a comfortable and familiar person in the White House.

After his reelection in November 1940, Roosevelt became much bolder in mobilizing the United States for war. The following month he delivered his historic "Arms for Democracy" speech in which he proposed the Lend-Lease program. With Britain running out of money, this program would provide a continued supply of arms without Britain having to pay cash. In March 1941 Congress responded with passage of the Lend-Lease Act. In August 1941 Roosevelt met with British leader Winston Churchill (1874–1965) on a U.S. naval ship off Newfoundland, Canada. They signed the Atlantic Charter, which defined the war aims of the two nations. Following the German invasion of the Soviet Union, Roosevelt extended the Lend-Lease program to the Soviets in November. Meanwhile, Roosevelt also placed a strict trade embargo (ban on trade with a foreign nation) on Japan and froze Japanese assets in the United States.

War arrives

War finally arrived at the doorstep of the United States on December 7, 1941, when Japanese forces carried out a surprise bombing attack on U.S. military bases at Pearl Harbor, Hawaii. The attack killed more than two thousand American military personnel and destroyed many military ships and airplanes. Within the next few days the United States plunged into war on two fronts: Europe and the Pacific.

For the next few years Roosevelt provided firm, steady inspirational leadership to the nation while leaving the detailed orchestration of war to a group of highly capable military and corporate leaders. These included Republicans

Henry L. Stimson (1867–1950; see entry) as secretary of war and Frank Knox (1874–1944) as secretary of the navy. The president wanted to create a more bipartisan (involving both political parties) approach to the war effort. As he had during the Great Depression, Roosevelt created numerous temporary war agencies to coordinate activities. Roosevelt's participation focused more on the larger strategic decision making such as emphasizing the war in Europe first over the Pacific front and attacking German forces first in North Africa rather than in Europe. The president also authorized the Manhattan Project early in the war to develop the atomic bomb, later used by President Harry S. Truman (1884–1972; served 1945–53) to end the war with Japan in August 1945.

The invasion of North Africa began in November 1942. Allied forces pushed the fight from there into Sicily and Italy by the summer of 1943. Meanwhile, beginning with the battle of the Coral Sea in May 1942, U.S. forces fought from island to island across the Pacific. Roosevelt ended any further efforts at

President Franklin D. Roosevelt sits between French generals Henri Giraud (left) and Charles de Gaulle (right center) along with British Prime Minister Winston Churchill (right) during the Casablanca Conference in Morocco, January 1943. *Courtesy of the FDR Library.*

domestic reform legislation and provided little resistance in 1943 when Congress ended several New Deal programs. The massive U.S. wartime spending, converting production of consumer goods to wartime materials, essentially ended the Great Depression and brought full employment.

Roosevelt met with Churchill again in January 1943 in Casablanca, Morocco, and once more in November 1943 in Tehran, Iran. At Tehran they met with Soviet leader Joseph Stalin (1879–1953) for the first time. Roosevelt and Churchill promised Stalin they would invade France by spring of 1944 and Stalin promised to attack Japan once the European war was over. The Soviets could also keep parts of Poland that it had recently captured in pushing German forces back.

Postwar concerns

By mid-1944 eventual victory was taking shape. Roosevelt began to look more toward the nature of the world following war. Based on the Atlantic Charter, twenty-six nations signed the United Nations Declaration. In July 1944 he hosted an international conference at Bretton Woods, New Hampshire, to plan for a postwar world economy. Out of the conference came the International Monetary Fund and an international bank to assist European and Asian nations in their recovery from war.

Still believing government had a responsibility toward the economic security of American citizens, Roosevelt played a role in the Servicemen's Readjustment Act of 1944, more commonly known as the GI Bill. The bill provided generous housing, educational, and other benefits to war veterans.

By the November 1944 elections, Allied troops had regained most of France and captured all the Pacific islands east of Japan including the Philippines. They were closing in on both German and Japanese soil. Nevertheless, the public felt uncertain about postwar conditions, both the domestic economy and international relations with the Soviet Union. As a result, Roosevelt won reelection again in November 1944 for a fourth term. However, Roosevelt was suffering from advanced arteriosclerosis (heart disease), and his health was markedly fading. In January 1945 Roosevelt met with British leader Winston Churchill and Soviet leader Joseph Stalin at

Yalta in the Soviet Union to determine postwar occupation of Germany and create an international organization to help avoid future wars. Roosevelt was visibly in very poor health at the meetings.

In April 1945, with the war in Europe winding down, Roosevelt traveled to his spa in Warm Springs for a much-needed rest. On April 12, while an artist painted his portrait, Roosevelt suddenly collapsed from a massive cerebral hemor-rhage (bleeding in the brain). He died only a few hours later. The nation was plunged into profound grief as one of its most beloved leaders had passed away.

A giant figure

Roosevelt is recognized as one of the great world fig-ures of the twentieth century. He served an unprecedented twelve years as U.S. president, leading the nation through two major prolonged crises, the Great Depression and World War II. Roosevelt established an expanded view of government—that it should provide an economic safety net for its citizens in times of trouble.

However, some important issues were not addressed during Roosevelt's time in office. Civil rights issues received little attention and racial discrimination continued largely unchallenged. The armed forces remained racially segregated throughout World War II. In addition, 110,000 Japanese Americans were placed in internment camps from 1942 to 1944 despite lack of any evidence of disloyalty to the United States. The United States also made minimal efforts to assist European Jews trying to flee from the oppression of Nazi Germany in the late 1930s. Nonetheless, Roosevelt immedi-ately stopped the dramatic decline of the national economy in the 1930s and successfully guided the nation through a mas-sive and complex world war. He laid the foundation for the postwar international order, including formation of the United Nations.

Numerous tributes to Roosevelt include the Roosevelt Presidential Library built near his home at Hyde Park, New York. His image was placed on the dime in U.S. currency, and the Roosevelt Monument was dedicated in Washington, D.C., in 1997.

For More Information

Books

Freidel, Frank. *Franklin D. Roosevelt: A Rendezvous with Destiny.* Boston: Little, Brown, 1990.

Goodwin, Doris Kearns. *No Ordinary Time: Franklin and Eleanor Roosevelt, the Home Front in World War II.* New York: Simon & Schuster, 1994.

Meacham, Jon. *Franklin and Winston: An Intimate Portrait of an Epic Friendship.* New York: Random House, 2003.

Roosevelt, Eleanor. *The Autobiography of Eleanor Roosevelt.* New York: Da Capo Press, 1992.

Web sites

Franklin D. Roosevelt Library and Museum. http://www.fdrlibrary.marist.edu (accessed on July 25, 2004).

Henry L. Stimson

Born September 21, 1867
New York, New York
Died October 20, 1950
Huntington, New York

Secretary of war, diplomat

Henry L. Stimson became one of the most respected U.S. leaders during World War II (1939–45). Many considered Stimson the chief architect for Allied victory in the war by organizing the U.S. war effort, including home front mobilization. Stimson also played a major role in preparing Americans on the home front for future sacrifices. As a result, the United States had the best-equipped army in the world. Stimson was outspoken in taking a strong stand against German military expansion in Europe. He was one of the most influential policy makers of the twentieth century as the United States emerged as a great military and economic world leader. However, his inspired foreign policy was tempered by a strong racial bias. This bias was reflected by his resistance to racially integrate the armed forces during the war and to insist on the internment of Japanese Americans in the western United States.

"If you are going to try to go to war . . . in a capitalist country, you have got to let business make money . . . or business won't work."

Henry L. Stimson.
Getty Images. Reproduced by permission.

A privileged childhood

Henry Lewis Stimson was born on September 21, 1867, in New York City, only two years after the end of the American

Civil War (1861–65). His father was Lewis Atterbury Stimson, a Wall Street stockbroker. His mother was Candace Wheeler. In 1871 Lewis left the New York Stock Exchange and took the family to Europe, where he studied medicine for the next three years. Upon his completion, they returned to the United States but Henry's mother soon died. As a result, Henry was raised by his grandparents. He received an excellent education. At age thirteen Henry entered the Phillips Academy in Andover, Massachusetts, and from there attended Yale University. He graduated in 1888 and entered Harvard Law School, graduating in 1890 with a master's degree.

Henry Stimson returned to New York City, where he was admitted to the New York bar in 1891 and became a Wall Street lawyer. He joined the law firm of Root and Clark. Elihu Root (1845–1937), a major influence on Stimson, would become secretary of war and secretary of state between 1897 and 1909. Two years after joining the firm in 1893, Stimson married Mabel White, a girlfriend from Yale. They would have no children in their fifty-seven years of marriage.

A life of public service

While pursuing his law practice, Stimson became active in Republican politics. In 1906 President Theodore Roosevelt (1858–1919; served 1901–09) appointed Stimson U.S. attorney for the southern district of New York. Serving for three years, Stimson pursued historic antitrust cases and became a supporter of progressive politics. Those who supported progressivism believed it was proper to use governmental powers to solve national economic and social issues. Rising quickly in politics, Stimson was selected the Republican candidate for governor of New York in 1910. However, he did not prove to be an effective campaigner. Stimson had a conservative and cold personality, and he did not relate well to voters. He could be harsh and abrupt with his peers. He lost badly in this, his only political campaign.

In 1911 President William Howard Taft (1857–1930; served 1909–13) appointed Stimson secretary of war. Stimson would serve five presidents in various capacities from 1911 to 1945. While secretary of war, he modernized the military organization, a move that would greatly help mobilization in

World War I (1914–18) and World War II. With the entrance of Democrat Woodrow Wilson (1856–1924; served 1913–21) into the White House in 1913, Stimson returned to his private law practice. When the United States entered World War I in 1917, Stimson, at forty-nine years of age, volunteered for military service. He became an army artillery officer who saw active duty in France. Stimson attained the rank of colonel before the war's end. He once again returned to his law practice as a corporate lawyer on Wall Street. Stimson benefited from the economic boom times of the 1920s, making a substantial income.

However, public service soon came calling again. In 1927 President Calvin Coolidge (1872–1933; served 1923–29) selected Stimson for a diplomatic mission to Nicaragua to resolve a civil war. He was able to help the two sides reach a settlement though fighting lingered for a few more years. Seen as a great success, Stimson was named governor general of the Philippines in 1928. Dedicated to the economic development of the islands, he became a very popular governor for the one year he was there. In 1929 President Herbert Hoover (1874–1964; served 1929–33) appointed Stimson as secretary of state.

Secretary of war, again

When Democrat **Franklin D. Roosevelt** (1882–1945; served 1933–45; see entry) took over the White House in 1933, Stimson once again returned to his law practice. From the beginning in the late 1930s, Stimson was one of the few higher U.S. statesmen who called for opposition to German expansion in Europe and for a strengthened U.S. military. Others, particularly fellow Republicans, took positions of isolationism (avoiding foreign commitments or involvement). He was a leading member of the Committee to Defend America by Aiding the Allies. Roosevelt agreed with Stimson's views and in 1940 appointed the Republican Stimson secretary of war once again. Roosevelt also appointed Republican Frank Knox (1874–1944) secretary of the navy. The president was trying to build bipartisan (from both major political parties) support for the upcoming war effort. Stimson accepted with two conditions: he would not be expected to participate in home front politics and he could select his own assistants.

U.S. Secretary of War Henry Stimson, blindfolded, pulls numbers in a lottery for the first peacetime military draft in U.S. history, October 29, 1940. Stimson took a strong stand against German military expansion in Europe and was instrumental in organizing the U.S. war effort, including mobilization of the military and home front.
AP/Wide World Photos. Reproduced by permission.

Stimson began work in his new position on July 10, 1940. His first action as war secretary was to seek establishment of a selective service system, the first peacetime draft (mandatory enrollment in the armed services) in U.S. history. Stimson supported Roosevelt in aiding foreign countries, first with the Destroyers for Bases program announced in September 1940 and then the Lend-Lease program that Roosevelt first announced in his December 29, 1940, "Arsenal of Democracy" speech. (Under the Lend-Lease program, Allied nations, who were quickly running out of money, could purchase military goods from the United States on credit instead of paying by cash, as they had been up until that time.) Congress passed the Lend-Lease Act in March 1941. When German forces invaded the Soviet Union in June 1941, Stimson pressed Roosevelt to begin shipping aid to Britain. Stimson wanted Roosevelt to go to the public and prepare them for war. Roosevelt would sign the selective service bill on September 16, 1940. As a result, the army expanded to

1.4 million servicemen. Stimson also pressed Congress hard for providing businesses financial incentives to mobilize. Being a well-known Republican favoring Roosevelt's desire to send military aid to Britain and to institute a military draft, Stimson helped the Democratic president's cause for selling Congress and the public on the need to prepare for war.

To conduct the war effort, Stimson assembled a top team of experts to get U.S. industrial mobilization underway on the home front. His team included Robert Patterson (1891–1952), John J. McCloy (1895–1989), Robert A. Lovett (1895–1986), and Harvey Bundy (1888–1963). Patterson was assistant secretary in charge of army procurement of supplies. McCloy assisted in general, tackling various problems as they appeared. Lovett oversaw the air force, from home front production of warplanes to their use in combat. Bundy worked as liaison with various congressional committees and served as personal advisor to Stimson. Despite his cool mannerisms in public, Stimson was noted for his integrity and inspired loyalty and even affection from those who knew him well.

War begins

When war did break out for the United States with the bombing of Pearl Harbor, Hawaii, on December 7, 1941, Stimson was seventy-four years of age. Pearl Harbor caught him by surprise. He knew from intelligence reports that a Japanese attack on U.S. interests was imminent, but he believed it would occur in the west Pacific, such as the Philippine Islands. He underestimated Japan's capabilities and vowed not to underestimate the Japanese again.

As a result, Stimson pushed for the internment of all Japanese Americans living on the West Coast of the United States. He received presidential approval on February 19, 1942, to evacuate 112,000 Japanese Americans to hastily constructed relocation camps in remote desert areas further inland. He steadfastly held to the belief that they posed a danger to the American home front, even though no Japanese American was ever charged with a war crime. He also believed racial integration of the military would be too disruptive during the time of war. So he decided racially segregated units would be used, with blacks serving only under white officers.

Robert Patterson

As the newly appointed secretary of war, Henry L. Stimson began war mobilization of U.S. industry in 1940. He selected Robert Patterson (1891–1952) as a top assistant. Patterson resigned a federal judge position to become assistant secretary of war. He and Stimson knew each other well. Both were Harvard graduates and Republicans. They also both served in World War I in the same army division in France. During the 1930s they formed an even closer friendship while opposing isolationism in America.

Born in Glens Falls, New York, Patterson followed his father's footsteps into the legal profession by studying law at Harvard. Following graduation, he joined a prestigious law firm headed by Elihu Root (1845–1937), who had been secretary of war and secretary of state between 1897 and 1909. Influenced by Root, Patterson was a strong supporter for national defense. Following World War I, Patterson established a successful New York law firm and did financially well through the economic boom years of the 1920s. In 1930 President Herbert Hoover (1874–1964; served 1929–33)

appointed Patterson as a judge to the U.S. District Court of Southern New York. In 1939 President Franklin D. Roosevelt (1882–1945; served 1933–45) appointed Patterson to the U.S. Court of Appeals.

During World War II, Patterson rose to be undersecretary of war. From that position he oversaw the army's multibillion-dollar purchasing program, a highly important position throughout mobilization. Patterson believed military contracts should largely go to major corporations who were already prepared to launch into mass production of war materials. As a result, Patterson forged a strong relationship between the military and big business that persisted into the twenty-first century and greatly influenced American foreign policy. Like Stimson, he staunchly opposed racial segregation in the military services. Following the war, Patterson successfully pushed for all military services to be combined into one department, the newly formed Department of Defense, in 1947. That same year, Patterson resigned from public service and returned to a private law practice. Only five years later, in 1952, he was killed in a commercial airliner crash.

During the war, Stimson wanted tight security on war operations and viewed civilians (those not in the military) in government with suspicion. He was often impolite to the press and particularly to **Elmer Davis** (1890–1958; see entry), head of the government's Office of War Information (OWI). The OWI was in charge of disseminating information about the war to the American public. Stimson saw little value in informing the public on the home front. Stimson and Davis persisted in strong contention, with Stimson holding the upper hand. Even the facts concerning the results of the Pearl Harbor attack were not disclosed for a year. Roosevelt, however, would routinely back up Stimson when conflicts with others were raised to the president.

While his top-notch aides carried out mobilization efforts, Stimson took the lead in the Manhattan Project, the top secret project to build the atomic bomb. It was so secret, Stimson was the person to inform Harry S. Truman (1884–1972; served 1945–53) of it when Truman became president in 1945 following the sudden death of Franklin Roosevelt. Stimson played a major role in the decision to drop two atomic bombs on Japanese cities in August 1945, ending the war.

Once the war was over, Stimson resigned from his post and retired on his seventy-eighth birthday on September 21, 1945, immediately after the Japanese surrender. Truman awarded Stimson the Distinguished Service Medal that day. He returned to his estate on Long Island, where he lived for the last five years of his life. Stimson died on October 20, 1950, in Huntington, New York.

For More Information

Books

Hodgson, Godfrey. *The Colonel: The Life and Wars of Henry Stimson, 1867–1950*. New York: Alfred A. Knopf, 1990.

Morison, Elting E. *Turmoil and Tradition: A Study of the Life and Times of Henry Stimson*. Boston: Houghton Mifflin, 1960.

Schmitz, David F. *Henry L. Stimson: The First Wise Man*. Wilmington, DE: SR Books, 2001.

Stimson, Henry, and McGeorge Bundy. *On Active Service in Peace and War*. New York: Harper, 1948.

Web sites

The Henry L. Stimson Center. http://www.stimson.org (accessed on July 26, 2004).

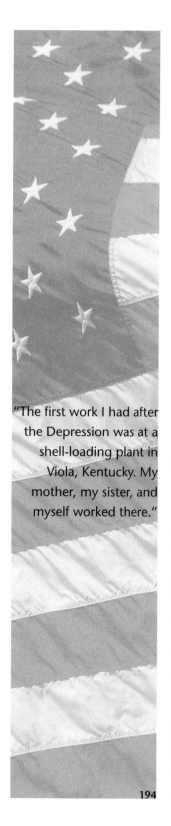

Peggy Terry

Born c. 1922

Factory worker

Prior to World War II (1939–45), women usually only worked outside of the home following the completion of their education until marriage. However, as twelve million men joined the military in the early 1940s, critical industrial jobs faced a worker shortage. Peggy Terry was one of nineteen million women who found work on the home front during the war years. Not only did the work vastly improve women's personal financial condition, but it opened the doors much wider for the acceptance of women in the workplace in America.

An early life of need

Peggy Terry was born around 1922 to a family that lived in poverty for most of her early years. Her mother was born in Kentucky and her father in Oklahoma. Her father fought in World War I (1914–18) as a machine gunner and was left emotionally scarred from the experience. Peggy was born only a few years after the war. For the next fifteen years, the family moved back and forth between Kentucky and Oklahoma. While living in Oklahoma between 1929 and 1936, they experienced the worst of the Great Depression (1929–41). The Great Depression, beginning in the fall of 1929 and lasting through the 1930s, was the worst economic crisis in U.S. history. Close to a quarter of the nation's workforce was unemployed. Many Americans did not have enough food. For those in Oklahoma and other parts of the Midwest, the Depression also included surviving the severe drought years of the early 1930s. The region became known as the Dust Bowl.

By 1937 Peggy's father lost his job, so they returned to Paducah, Kentucky. In Kentucky her father worked at times in the mines and was active in the workers' unions. Peggy married around 1937. Her husband, Bill, worked for the Works Progress Administration (WPA), digging ditches for city water lines. She was fifteen years of age and he was sixteen. For the next three years they traveled around hitchhiking. Peggy was expecting their first child while on the road. They found jobs as migrant workers, picking oranges, grapefruit, and lemons in the Rio Grande Valley of south Texas.

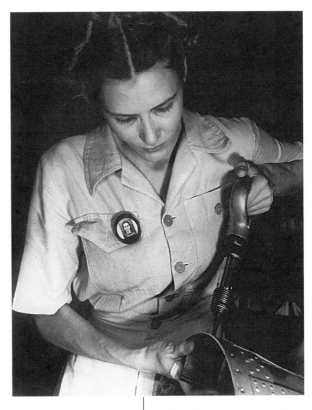

A female factory worker is shown working at the Naval Air Base in Corpus Christi, Texas, in 1942. Mobilization for war allowed thousands of women the opportunity to hold jobs outside the home and contribute to home front activities. *Courtesy of the FDR Library.*

Work comes to the home front

Peggy and Bill had returned to Paducah when mobilization of industry for war began in 1940. She was eighteen years old and her husband was nineteen. Her mother, a sister, and Peggy found jobs at a shell-loading plant in Viola, Kentucky, not far from Paducah. They worked different shifts at the factory so they could take care of children at home. After having no steady income through the Great Depression years, the thirty-two-dollar-a-week job seemed a godsend. They could once again buy new clothes and shoes, pay rent, and regularly put food on the table. It was the first job other than agricultural fieldwork that her mother had ever held. War mobilization on the home front brought a vast improvement to their lives.

Rosie the Riveter

Women like Peggy Terry who worked in America's factories during World War II (1939–45) attracted considerable national attention. At the time, it was thought a novelty for women to work in industrial jobs. Labeled "Rosie the Riveters," they worked in aircraft construction, shipbuilding, munitions manufacturing, and other related war industry jobs. They became glamorized in the media and the subject of posters as doing their part for the war. Noted artist **Norman Rockwell** (1894–1978; see entry) created the most memorable depiction of Rosie for the cover of the May 29, 1943, issue of *The Saturday Evening Post* (see photo on page 161).

Prior to the surprise Japanese attack on Pearl Harbor, Hawaii, in December 1941, few women worked in industry. By early 1944, 2,690,000 women were employed in the war industries. They comprised nearly 35 percent of all industry workers in the United States. No longer could people claim that women could not do mechanical work.

Thousands actually did work as riveters and welders in the war plants. Hundreds of thousands of women worked in shipyards across the country riveting sections of ships together. However, they worked in many other kinds of positions as

Most Americans could not recite the formal reasons President **Franklin D. Roosevelt** (1882–1945; served 1933–45; see entry) had given for going to war. They just knew that war involving the United States had been declared in some far-off location. They were essentially protecting the way of life that they knew. Peggy Terry was no different, particularly since she did not even have a radio in order to keep up with current events. Despite their disconnection, many Americans knew that the Germans and Japanese were their enemies. They were particularly suspicious of the Japanese, whose racial and cultural differences made European Americans uncomfortable. Terry saw local people destroy any items they owned that were made in Japan.

Terry also saw the hazards of factory work in a war industry. There were explosives, detonators, and hazardous materials, such as chemicals used in the explosives and cleaning substances used in the final production stages. Terry recounted well. At munitions factories, like the one where Peggy Terry first worked, women operated machines that made gun parts, and they wired fuses for bombs and filled bullets with powder. Others greased and painted gun barrels in their final production before shipment overseas to the battlefront. Terry next worked in the aircraft industry. At many aircraft plants, such as Douglas Aircraft, more than 40 percent of the workers were women during the war. Like Terry, many women moved beyond assembly line work to testing the airplane's systems. In steel mills, women rebuilt furnaces. It was found that women, because of their smaller hands, were often better able than men to assemble tiny parts in machine shops for precision aircraft instruments.

The Rosie the Riveter symbol lived on for decades, later representing the extensive role women played in the American home front war effort. When the war ended, millions of men returned from active military service seeking jobs. Women, especially those in the traditionally male-oriented factory jobs, were commonly among the first workers laid off as industry cut back war production and transitioned to producing consumer goods again. Most women employed in aircraft, shipbuilding, and munitions manufacturing during the war were quickly let go after the war.

how many women came away with their hair, skin, and even eyeballs discolored from the persistent exposure to chemicals. Some experienced breathing problems from the fumes in the air. Their noses and throats often burned. Though working conditions were poor, Terry knew little of union activities to improve their conditions.

Despite these harsh working conditions, the workers shared a pride in their accomplishments. Terry's munitions factory received a navy award for its efforts. A navy band came to play at the award ceremony.

Work at an aircraft factory

Terry's grandfather worked for the railroads and retired to Jackson, Michigan. After receiving word from her grandfather about the handsome wages for aircraft factory workers in Michigan, Terry moved there. She found a job testing airplane

Women operate hydraulic presses that form sheet metal parts for war planes at a factory in Inglewood, California. Like Peggy Terry, many women, despite terrible working conditions, went to work in such factories to support the war effort and earn a living. *Courtesy of the FDR Library.*

radios and made ninety dollars a week. It was a big increase from the munitions factory work. In Michigan, Terry discovered a whole different world than she had known in Kentucky. She worked with many eastern European immigrants who were very involved in union activity. Like many Americans, life on the home front as well as on foreign battlefields was a major education. Terry saw a larger world with greater social and cultural diversity. Like other home front workers, her expectations increased about a future life in the United States, including financial security.

While Peggy Terry worked in the factories, her husband, Bill, was a paratrooper in the military. Bill saw considerable action in North Africa, France, and Germany, making twenty-six parachute jumps in all. Like Terry's father from World War I, Bill came back from war in Europe emotionally scarred. He now smoked, drank too much, and at times physically abused the family. Terry claimed she lost her faith in religion because of the war's effects. Many of her childhood friends had died fighting in the war.

Nonetheless, Terry was financially considerably better off than before the war. As so many young brides did immediately following the war, Terry became pregnant shortly after Bill's return from the service, contributing to the phenomenon known as the baby boom. Following the war, Peggy and Bill settled into a small apartment in Chicago, Illinois.

Although most women were laid off from their war-related jobs soon after the war to make room for returning servicemen, the idea of women in the workplace became more socially accepted thanks to the contributions made by working women during World War II.

For More Information

Books

Gluck, Sherna Berger. *Rosie the Riveter Revisited: Women, the War, and Social Change*. Boston: Twayne Publishers, 1987.

Hartmann, Susan M. *The Home Front and Beyond: American Women in the 1940s*. Boston: Twayne Publishers, 1982.

Terkel, Studs. *The Good War: An Oral History of World War II*. New York: New Press, 1997.

Zeinert, Karen. *Those Incredible Women of World War II*. Brookfield, CT: Millbrook Press, 1994.

Web sites

Rosie the Riveter and Other Women World War II Heroes. http://www.u.arizona.edu/~kari/rosie.htm (accessed on July 26, 2004).

Rosie the Riveter Trust. http://www.rosietheriveter.org (accessed on July 26, 2004).

Where to Learn More

Books

Bailey, Ronald H. *The Home Front, U.S.A.* Alexandria, VA: Time-Life Books, 1977.

Bernstein, Mark, and Alex Lubertozzi. *World War II on the Air: Edward R. Murrow and the Voices That Carried the War Home.* Naperville, IL: Sourcebooks, 2003.

Carl, Ann B. *A Wasp Among Eagles.* Washington, DC: Smithsonian Institution Press, 1999.

Cooper, Michael L. *Remembering Manzanar: Life in a Japanese Relocation Camp.* New York: Clarion Books, 2002.

Cooper, Michael L. *Fighting For Honor: Japanese Americans and World War II.* New York: Clarion Books, 2000.

Daniels, Roger. *Prisoners Without Trial: Japanese Americans in World War II.* New York: Hill and Wang, 1993.

Freidel, Frank. *Franklin D. Roosevelt: A Rendezvous with Destiny.* New York: Little, Brown & Co., 1990.

Fremon, David K. *Japanese-American Internment in American History.* Springfield, NJ: Enslow Publishers, 1996.

Gilbert, Bill. *They Also Served: Baseball and the Home Front, 1941–1945.* New York: Crown Publishers, 1992.

Gluck, Sherna Berger. *Rosie the Riveter Revisited: Women, the War, and Social Change.* Boston: Twayne Publishers, 1987.

Goodwin, Doris Kearns. *No Ordinary Time: Franklin and Eleanor Roosevelt, the Home Front in World War II.* New York: Simon & Schuster, 1994.

Greene, Bob. *Once Upon a Town: The Miracle of the North Platte Canteen.* New York: William Morrow, 1992.

Hartmann, Susan M. *The Home Front and Beyond: American Women in the 1940s.* Boston: Twayne Publishers, 1982.

Heide, Robert. *Home Front America: Popular Culture of the World War II Era.* San Francisco: Chronicle Books, 1995.

Hoopes, Roy. *When The Stars Went To War: Hollywood and World War II.* New York: Random House, 1994.

Lingeman, Richard R. *Don't You Know There's a War On? The American Home Front, 1941–1945.* New York: G. P. Putnam's Sons, 1970.

Nathan, Amy. *Yankee Doodle Gals: Women Pilots of World War II.* Washington, DC: National Geographic Society, 2001.

New York Times. *Page One: The Front Page History of World War II as Presented in the New York Times.* New York: Galahad Books, 1996.

Panchyk, Richard. *World War II For Kids: A History With 21 Activities.* Chicago: Chicago Review Press, 2002.

Schickel, Richard. *Good Morning, Mr. Zip Zip Zip: Movies, Memory, and World War II.* Chicago: Ivan R. Dee, 2003.

Schomp, Virginia. *World War II: Letters From the Homefront.* New York: Benchmark Books, 2002.

Stanley, Jerry. *I Am An American: The True Story of Japanese Interment.* New York: Crown, 1994.

Takaki, Ronald T. *Double Victory: A Multicultural History of America in World War II.* Boston: Little, Brown and Company, 2000.

Terkel, Studs. *The Good War: An Oral History of World War Two.* New York: Pantheon Books, 1984.

Tunnell, Michael O. *The Children of Topaz: The Story of a Japanese-American Internment Camp.* New York: Holiday House, 1996.

Warren, James R. *The War Years: A Chronicle of Washington State in World War II.* Seattle: University of Washington Press, 2000.

Winkler, Allan M. *Home Front U.S.A.: America During World War II.* Arlington Heights, IL: H. Davidson, 1986.

Zeinert, Karen. *Those Incredible Women of World War II.* Brookfield, CT: The Millbrook Press, 1994.

Web Sites

The Army Nurse Corps. http://www.army.mil/cmh-pg/books/wwii/72-14/72-14.htm.

Army Women's Museum, Fort Lee, Virginia. http://www.awm.lee.army.mil.

Civil Air Patrol. http://www.cap.gov/about/history.html.

Coast Guard Auxiliary History. http://www.uscg.mil/hq/g-cp/history/Auxiliary%20History.html.

"Dorothea Lange and the Relocation of the Japanese." *Museum of the City of San Francisco.* http://www.sfmuseum.org/hist/lange.html.

Fly Girls. PBS Online. American Experience. http://www.pbs.org/wgbh/amex/flygirls.htm.

Japanese American National Museum. http://www.janm.org.

Rosie the Riveter Trust. http://www.rosietheriveter.org.

United Services Organization. http://www.uso.org.

The WASP WWII Museum. Avenger Field, Sweetwater, Texas. http://www.waspwwii.org/museum/home.htm.

The Women's Army Corps: A Commemoration of World War II Service. http://www.army.mil/cmh-pg/brochures/wac/wac.htm.

World War II Era WAVES. http://www.history.navy.mil/photos/prs-tpic/females/wave-ww2.htm.

Index

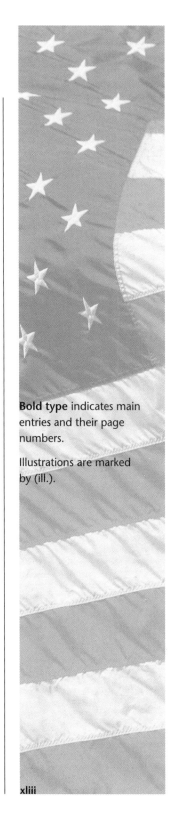

Bold type indicates main entries and their page numbers.

Illustrations are marked by (ill.).

N